MW01032601

A 'FAMILY' BUSINESS

The Life And Times Of
Joey 'The Fixer' Silvestri

JOE SILVESTRI
DENNIS N. GRIFFIN

WILDBLUE
PRESS

WildBluePress.com

A 'FAMILY' BUSINESS published by:

WILDBLUE PRESS
P.O. Box 102440
Denver, Colorado 80250

WILDBLUE PRESS is registered at the U.S. Patent and Trademark Offices.

ISBN 978-1-948239-92-9   Trade Paperback
ISBN 978-1-948239-93-6   eBook

Interior Formatting/Book Cover Design by Elijah Toten
www.totencreative.com

A 'FAMILY' BUSINESS

The Life And Times Of
Joey 'The Fixer' Silvestri

DEDICATION

This book is dedicated to my family with all my love.

My wonderful wife Babe, my daughter Linda,
and my son Joseph and his wife Lisa.

My grandchildren: Joseph and Antoinette, Vanessa and
her husband Anthony, and Christopher and his wife Liz.

And my great-grandchildren: Nino,
Michael, Alexia, and Christopher.

TABLE OF CONTENTS

PREFACE

I was introduced to Joe Silvestri by our mutual friend Tony Napoli. Tony is the son of the late Genovese crime family capo, James "Jimmy Nap" Napoli. Jimmy was highly respected by all five of the New York City families. So much so that for years he ran the largest illegal gambling operation in the country on their behalf. I think Tony is best described as "old school." He believes in being loyal and has little tolerance for those he feels are not. When he suggested to me that Joe had some interesting stories to tell, I paid attention.

The beauty of a recommendation from Tony is that no further vetting is necessary in regard to trustworthiness. You don't make it onto Tony's friend list unless you are a "standup" guy. I knew that before I ever talked with Joe, and I think Joe felt the same about me. When I did speak with Joe, it did not take very long for me to understand why Tony liked him. I agreed to write his story.

Over many hours of recorded conversations, Joe captivated me with his experiences while working at The Copacabana, meeting entertainers such as Tom Jones, Dean Martin, Jerry Lewis, and Frank Sinatra. He and Sammy Davis became close friends. He also met celebrity customers from the entertainment and sports worlds. His story about the "basebrawl" incident involving several New York Yankees players—including Billy Martin, Mickey Mantle and Hank

Bauer—was fascinating. The Copa was frequented by some of the top mobsters of the day as well, whom Joe refers to as "VIPs." Joe got involved with the rackets himself in the form of illegal gambling and was quite successful at it.

A major turning point in his life came when he met a businessman named Frank Cioli, who owned the famous Grimaldi's pizza chain. Their relationship started out positive and Joe became manager to a couple of the stores. However, as time passed, Joe came to realize he had partnered with a scoundrel. Frank pulled some very dirty deals on Joe and several of his other business associates. It was a rather disappointing ending for Joe.

Despite that, I enjoyed writing the book and developing a relationship with Joe. He is truly a standup guy.

Please note that some of the names appearing in this book have been changed to protect the identities of certain individuals.

Denny Griffin

INTRODUCTION

My name is Joseph Silvestri. My mother called me Joseph, but to most everybody else I was Joe or Joey. I was born in Astoria, Queens, on May 1, 1932, and had five brothers and two sisters. When I was six, we moved to Jackson Heights, also in Queens. We were about the only Italian family there at the time. I'd say I had a normal childhood and was an average or above student.

If I had to name my biggest fault as a kid and young adult, I'd say it was my penchant for using my fists. I was quick to fight and was pretty good at it. I wasn't particularly big, but I packed a wallop that broke some jaws and noses over the years. That talent—if that's the right word—came in handy on some occasions and caused problems other times.

After an abbreviated stint in the US Air Force in 1949, I spent several years working as a bartender or bouncer at various clubs in New York City, including three years at the world-famous Copacabana. I also worked some of the biggest illegal blackjack and poker games in the city. In that capacity, I met and became friends with many of the greats in the entertainment industry, as well as famous sports figures. I had contact with a number of people from the other side of the law too—organized crime. In this book I'll refer to them as "very important people" or "VIPs."

The stories I'll share with you are all true, and in most cases, this may very well be the first time you've heard of them. In those you may have heard of before, such as the 1957 brawl at the Copa involving several New York Yankees players, I'll provide inside details from my position as an eyewitness and participant.

You may find some of my accounts to be serious, humorous, or simply informative. My hope is you will find them all entertaining.

1 : FISTICUFFS

One of my early memories is when I graduated from grade school to high school. I was excited because I was in the chorus and we were going to sing on stage during the ceremony. I wasn't much of a cut-up, but I had two friends who were. Before we went on stage, the three of us were talking. Our music teacher told us to quiet down or we'd be excluded from singing. I became very quiet, but not my buddies.

The teacher said to me, "You're out of the exercise."

"Why? I didn't do anything."

"Okay, tell me who did."

I wouldn't give up my friends, and when the chorus was called on stage, I had to stay in my seat. *I was crushed.*

My mother and aunt were in the audience. When the diplomas were handed out and my name was called, they saw me walk up from the student section all by myself and join my classmates. On the way home, my mother asked me about it. I said, "Mama, I got a very special award and they wanted me to walk up there by myself, so I'd get full recognition."

She accepted that explanation and was proud of me.

I went on to Newtown High School in Elmhurst, Queens, where I met the girl who would become my wife a few years later. But my first day there started out with a problem. A kid I didn't know came up to me and said, "Are you Joe Silvestri?"

"Yeah, I am."

"When your older brother went to school here, he beat up my brother. Now I'm gonna kick your ass."

We went to an empty lot across the street from the school to duke it out. There was a big crowd of students around and most of them were rooting for me. I gave that kid a real whipping.

Teaching a bully a lesson was one thing, but I had trouble controlling when and on whom I used my fists. It was an issue that stayed with me most of my life.

* * *

When I turned seventeen in 1949, I quit school and joined the air force. It had just separated from the army and become its own branch. That was one of the biggest blunders I ever made in my life. I didn't know what real racial prejudice was until then.

I went for basic training in Texas, and then on to an assignment in Biloxi, Mississippi. My first problem in Biloxi came when I loaned a black kid in my outfit a civilian sweater I had. He told somebody where he got the sweater and about six guys converged on me in the barracks. They kept saying, "Where is that nigger lover?" They beat the hell out of me with their hands and feet. I sustained some injuries and still have stomach issues after all these years. Following that incident, I became rebellious—the air force wasn't for me and I wanted out.

One day when I was assigned to the company headquarters (HQ), the first sergeant gave me a letter to deliver to another HQ. On my way, I stopped by the field where the football team was practicing and didn't get the letter delivered until about an hour later. When I got back, my first sergeant was pissed off. "Where in the fuck have you been?"

"I got lost. I'd never been there before and couldn't find the right building."

"You lying guinea bastard!"

That was it. I hit him in the face so hard that his eyeglasses became embedded in the bridge of his nose. A bunch of guys grabbed me and took me to my barracks, and then to the stockade. I asked to see a priest and explained the situation to him. He was sympathetic and when I went to my court martial, I was given a general discharge under honorable conditions. I was out of the air force!

They gave me a ride into Biloxi in a Jeep. I was in the back with two MPs, and the first sergeant I'd hit was in the front. He turned to me and said, "If you ever come back on this base, I'll kill you!"

I said, "And if you ever come into town, *I'll* kill *you*."

We never saw each other again.

* * *

I liked Biloxi and stayed there for a while. I got involved with a woman several years older than me named Blossom. She taught me a lot about many things, including sex.

Next, I got a job at the Ballerina Club, which was no small thing being only seventeen. It was kind of like hitting the lottery would be today. What I didn't know at the time was that Blossom was related to the blackjack dealer there—a guy named Murphy. He'd taken a liking to me and she put in a good word for me, so he took me on.

After I was hired, Murphy started training me to deal blackjack. The first thing he did was take the ring off his pinky finger and hand it to me. "If you're going to deal blackjack, you can't have a naked hand. Wearing a ring will make you look more professional," he said. Murphy taught me a lot and he did it in a hurry. Before long, I was ready to go on my own. I broke in on quiet nights and afternoons.

One afternoon when it was really slow, I was playing solitaire when I heard a voice say, "Hey there, Joe Silvestri." I looked up and there was a kid in an air force uniform I knew from Corona. His name was Anthony. I got up from the table and we shook hands and embraced. He said he couldn't wait to get home on leave and tell all the guys that he'd seen me dealing blackjack in a big club. That gave me a real good feeling.

In addition to gambling, the Ballerina had a restaurant and dance hall with live music. They had a quartet with drums, bass, piano, and sax. They were all black and boy, could they wail. Sometimes, when it wasn't busy, I'd listen to them and dance with some of the beautiful women that hung around the club.

One night I met two gorgeous southern belles who looked like twins but weren't even related. I hooked up with one of them and we started seeing each other. It was great for a while, but then Blossom found out. I never knew what a southern temper was like until she went off on me. It was a living hell for a few days, but we got over it and I didn't stray any more.

* * *

One of the guys in the club I became good friends was named Big Pete. He was over six feet tall and weighed around 230 pounds. He was a moose of a man. He was known as the toughest guy in town and nobody messed with him.

I only saw Pete in action one time. We were in the pool room playing a game when a couple of air force guys came in with a few drinks under their belts. One of them challenged us to a game. Pete said we weren't interested. The smaller guy said, "What's the matter? Are you afraid we'll kick your ass?"

Pete said, "Take a walk."

Then the bigger guy got right in Pete's face. Pete hit him in the face with that huge right hand of his and knocked him across the floor and into the jukebox. He slammed into it so hard, several of the 45rpm records fell out of their spindles. Pete then kicked the smaller guy in the ass and threw him out the door. We beat it out of there before the MPs showed up.

Another time, Pete, his girlfriend, Blossom, and I went out to dinner in a neighboring town. Over dinner, I had only a couple of drinks, but Pete and his girl downed a lot of booze. When it was time to leave, I offered to drive but Pete refused. He got us back to Biloxi okay, then he turned the wrong way on a one-way street, pulled over, shut the car off, and started smooching it up with his girl.

It wasn't long before a police patrol car pulled up. The two cops got out and one went to each side of the car. It seemed the cop on the driver's side recognized Pete's car, but the cop on the other side pulled his gun out of its holster. The first cop tapped on Pete's window, but with the engine off, the power window wouldn't work and Pete couldn't open it.

I opened my door and asked the cop what he wanted. He said, "I just wanted to know if Pete's car broke down and he needs some help."

At that point, Pete got out of the car, and the cop with his gun drawn came around to the driver's side. The first cop told him, "Put your gun away. *Now*." The gun went back in its holster.

Pete assured the cops he wasn't having any problems. Everything was fine and he didn't need any help. They got back in their car and drove away. I couldn't believe it. No arrest for driving drunk, not even a ticket for going the wrong way on a one-way street.

Like I said: in Biloxi, nobody messed around with Big Pete.

* * *

Things were going good for me until one day when my mother called. She said, "Joey, Papa is very sick. You need to come home." The next day I boarded a train for New York and never looked back.

2 : INTRODUCTION TO THE GAMBLING LIFE

I arrived back in New York a couple of months short of my eighteenth birthday. My father was in the hospital, suffering from a bleeding ulcer. Although he was very weak, he held his own and eventually made a full recovery. He lived to be eighty-seven.

I didn't have a job and just hung around, visiting my father in the hospital and getting back in touch with my buddies. The latter took me to Newton High School, where I saw Babe, a girl I'd been kind of sweet on. I had sent her a letter from Biloxi, but she didn't respond. I walked over to her and asked why she didn't answer my letter.

She explained that she had heard I'd been seeing another girl before I entered the service, and under those circumstances, she didn't feel comfortable corresponding with me. I assured her I was not seeing anybody and asked her on a date. She stalled me; apparently not sure I was telling her the truth. It was only after her brother vouched for me that we began going out.

Babe lived in Corona Heights, Queens. Her neighborhood was comprised mostly of Italian families and I loved it there. The streets were lined with Italian bakeries, restaurants, butcher shops, cheese shops, and grocery stores. The Lemon Ice King of Corona made Italian ices to die for. I'll never forget those sights, tastes, and smells. Corona had something else I loved—gambling. It was a gambling town.

Babe and I were married on September 29, 1950. It was a small wedding with just a few of our family members present. We were short on money, so there was no honeymoon and we initially lived with my parents in Jackson Heights. A few months later, we were able to get an apartment back in Corona Heights, where I first got involved in the gambling business.

A guy from another section of Corona started coming around our neighborhood picking up numbers (for an illegal lottery sometimes referred to as the "numbers racket" or "policy racket"). I resented an outsider running numbers and making money on the locals. I took my concerns to the boss (a person with organized crime ties and lots of clout) of Corona Heights. He sided with me and I became the Corona numbers guy.

People quickly came to like and trust me, which was very important. Before long, I developed a nice business.

* * *

Every year on July 16, Our Lady of Mount Carmel Church put on a feast. There were all kinds of food and live music. Our event was small compared to the celebrations in Brooklyn and Harlem, but for our neighborhood, it was a major occurrence.

In the early 1950s, some of my friends and I were at the feast, eating clams, sausage and peppers, and having a great time.

One of the guys I was with liked to sing. He said to me, "Joey, do you think they'd let me up on the bandstand to sing a number with the band?"

"I don't see why not. I'll go ask."

I walked over to the bandstand and was trying to get the attention of the band leader when something poked me in the ribs. I swung around and a cop was standing there. It turned out he had asked me to move along, but with the music going, I didn't hear him. Thinking I was ignoring him, he'd used his stick to get my attention.

I don't know for sure what was in his mind when I turned toward him. Maybe he thought I was going to take a swing at him. Whatever the reason, he hit me right in the mouth so hard it knocked me back into the crowd. It was quite a punch. Fortunately for me, bumping into the spectators helped keep me on my feet.

I charged the cop and hit him in the face, sending him into the crowd (I later learned it required six stitches to close the cut where I hit him). He came back at me and we both went down.

More cops showed up. A sergeant had his foot on my face, pinning me to the ground. They arrested me and took me to the 112th Precinct. Still handcuffed, I was placed in a room with a chair and told to sit down.

My wife had called my brother Pat. He came to the station house and they allowed him to see me. Pat was an ex-Marine, very tough and very smart. He said, "Joey, they're going to kick the shit out of you, count on it. Whatever you do, don't raise a hand to them. Grab on to the sides of your chair if you have to, but don't fight with them."

Right after Pat left, a big cop came in and removed the cuffs. I figured the beating was going to start and was surprised when he walked out of the room. Just then, another, even bigger cop charged in and punched me in the head. I was hanging on to the chair. It tipped over and took me with it. That was just the beginning.

I was kept in that room overnight. With each shift change, a couple of the new arrivals paid me a visit and punched me around. Through it all, I did as Pat said. I never raised my hands.

When I went to court the next morning, I was hurting so bad I could hardly stand up. The judge, DA, and my assigned lawyer had a conference. Bail was set. I was able to post it and was released.

This kind of thing was all new to me, so after I got back to the neighborhood, I went to see a guy I had a lot of respect for—the local bookie. He not only took bets, he also ran a floating crap game (back then, we referred to shooting dice as "crap," not "craps") and card games. My fight with the cop was being talked about all over and he'd already heard about it.

He gave me some advice: enroll at the Delehanty Institute and take a police officer prep course. My initial reaction was not to do it. Then he said, "It's either that or they'll put you in jail."

I enrolled.

When I went back to court a couple of weeks later, my lawyer told the judge what a great young man I was. "Mr. Silvestri is a married man and a new father. He's attending the Delehanty Institute and is a future police officer."

The case was dismissed.

* * *

At the age of twenty-one, I was still picking up numbers and began working for my bookie friend at his nightly floating crap game. If you're not familiar with what a floating crap game is, it's a game held at various locations around the neighborhood—usually in an empty store or office space—and is moved to a different spot every few days to avoid attracting unwanted attention from the police, or neighbor complaints. Many of the players were well-known and couldn't afford to get pinched. So the location of the game had to be changed regularly.

My first job was what was called a "lugger." I'd lug (shuttle) players from a designated pickup location to the game and back. That way, gamblers weren't getting parking tickets or taking up the parking spaces of the area residents. Later, I became a doorman and earned a better pay.

I rented a vacant storefront at the corner of Corona Avenue and 51st Avenue and started running my own card games. I bought a shoeshine stand with elevated customer seats and placed it inside the store right behind the window, where I could sit, drink my coffee, and watch the activity on the street. Directly behind the stand, I put a floor-to-ceiling partition. If a passerby looked in the window, they could only see the stand and partition—not what was going on inside the store.

Back then, point rummy was very popular and, of course, poker. We also played gin rummy and pinochle. I made my money by taking five percent of every pot.

Sometimes, when I had enough customers—especially if a couple of them were big money guys—I ran an afternoon crap game. We didn't have a table and the dice were rolled on the floor. However, we offered the same basic bets and odds that were available in the Nevada casinos and most of the upper-end illegal games in the city. I never ran my game at night though, when it would have been in competition with my friend. That wouldn't have been right.

In the event a player went broke, I also did some shylocking. So if they wanted to keep gambling, they could borrow directly from me and not have to leave to get more money.

I remember, on one particular day, it was raining like hell and I had a good crap game started. It looked like it was going to be a good day for me.

Unfortunately, shortly after the game got going, two cops showed up. They were both on the pad of the neighborhood boss and shouldn't have bothered me. I was sure somebody had dropped a dime on me and the cops were there because of a specific complaint.

I knew one of the cops. I called him "Smiley" because he was the meanest, ugliest looking sonofabitch you'd ever see in your life. We didn't like each other.

However, I wasn't especially concerned for myself or the twenty or so guys in the store. I was more worried about my brother Pat, who was helping me out, my cousin Joey, and friend Jerry, who were both on parole. Pat was a legit guy and didn't need the grief of a gambling bust. Joey and Jerry would likely be in violation and could end up back in prison. *What was I gonna do?*

As luck would have it, when Smiley and his partner pulled up, they double-parked their car in front of the grocery store across the street from the game. A customer left the market and couldn't get his car out, so the driver laid on his horn. Smiley's partner left to move the patrol car, and Smiley leaned against the door to prevent anyone from opening it. That gave me the chance I needed. I grabbed

Smiley under his armpits from behind and threw him out the door. He lost his footing on the slippery sidewalk and fell facedown into a grassy area near the curb, which due to all the rain, it was just a big mud puddle.

Before Smiley could regain his feet, my place was empty. Nobody got arrested—not even me. Still, I knew I'd have to answer for my actions.

Two days later, the boss of the neighborhood called and said he wanted to see me. When I met him, he said Smiley had come to him and told him what happened. He said, "You're going to have to buy him and his partner a hat." That meant I had to give the two cops a hundred dollars each. I was mad as hell about it, but that's the way business was done.

The next day, I was sitting in my shoeshine chair when Smiley and his partner made their appearance. They were really busting my balls and trying to provoke me. I kept my composure and didn't say or do anything back. I'd already bought them one hat and wasn't going to put myself in a position where I'd have to buy them another.

3 : A ROUGH START

When I first got married, I worked a variety of jobs. One that I particularly liked was driving a truck in the garment district. My driver's license was suspended at the time due to a number of unpaid traffic tickets (I was kind of wild then and thought of those tickets as just pieces of paper that didn't require any action on my part), but the owner of the company arranged for me to get a restricted license that allowed me to drive only his truck.

The Copa was located at 10 East 60th Street and was on my route. It was already legendary and I had learned quite a bit about it. I knew its owner, Jules Podell, was recognized as a true genius in the nightclub and restaurant business. Other places copied him, and when some of the big hotels opened in Florida, they also followed his format.

As an example of Mr. Podell's business acumen, when he booked acts he thought were up-and-comers, he'd sign them to a two-year contract for a certain number of appearances. He paid them peanuts though, and many of them tried to get out of those contracts without success.

Even with the low pay, appearing at the Copa was still a good deal. If you were an entertainer and had the Copa on your résumé, you could work anywhere in America or Europe—and many of them became international stars. They included Sammy Davis, Paul Anka, Tom Jones, Vic

Damone, Jack Jones, Bobby Darin, Tony Bennett, Johnny Mathis, and the comedy team of Rowen & Martin.

The Copa was said by many to be the best value in the Big Apple. There was no admission fee, and customers were only required to spend a minimum of five dollars per person, which could be used on either food or beverage. You could dance to live big band music, see a complete show, take in three acts, and see the Copa Girls. The thought of working there and wearing a tux thrilled me.

* * *

The first time I got inside the Copa was when I had to deliver a case of carpet cleaning fluid. While I was waiting to get paid, I walked around and found myself in the showroom, where Tony Bennett was performing. I was in awe. Who would have thought that a few years later, I'd be walking Frank Sinatra out on that same floor? I certainly didn't.

About three years after making that delivery, I got a call from my brother-in-law, Leo. He said a boyhood friend of his was working at the Copa. Leo made a phone call for me and I eventually talked with Julie Pellerin, who worked the door at the Copa. We hit it off pretty good and he got me an interview with Mr. Podell. I didn't realize it then, but getting an interview with him was a pretty big deal.

I was twenty-four and a pretty good-looking young man, five-ten, and around 185 pounds. I went to my interview wearing a blue suit, with a white shirt and tie. Mr. Podell, who was probably in his fifties at the time, apparently took a liking to me and offered to hire me as a waiter. I told him I was no waiter, but he assured me it wasn't a big deal and not to worry about it. I reported for work the next day.

The main entrance was at street level. When you entered, the check room was straight ahead, and to the right was the famous Copa Lounge. Stairs on the left took you down to the basement, where the showroom was located. Also in the basement were two big kitchens, one with American cuisine, the other specializing in Chinese food. The Copa was known to have the best Chinese food in New York. There was also a big bar that served the showroom.

Down another level were the locker and changing rooms for the staff. Due to a lack of space, the entertainers changed in their hotel rooms and were ready to go on when they arrived for their gigs.

I was issued a white waiter's jacket with a red collar and cuffs, and gold buttons. I thought it was outlandish, but it was what it was. I was assigned to work upstairs in the lounge, which was good because I knew I wasn't ready to handle the showroom. I spent most of my first two shifts just walking around and doing absolutely nothing. That changed late on my second day though, which turned out to be my last day as a waiter.

At that time, call girls charged a hundred dollars a night. To help keep them under control, it was Copa policy that no woman could enter the lounge or showroom unescorted. So if they came in, they'd be with their date and not soliciting all the guys in the place.

This beautiful, very well-endowed girl came in with a guy who looked like a hayseed from cow country. A working girl and her trick. They sat down and I took their order—a split of champagne for her and a bottle of beer for him. I opened the beer and started pouring it into the guy's glass, but my gaze was fixed on that beautiful bosom across the table. I didn't realize the glass had a crack in it and the beer was running out onto the guy's lap. He started yelling. The manager came over and told me to leave the floor immediately. He did whatever he had to do to satisfy the pissed off customer, and then called me back in. I went, but already realized being a waiter wasn't for me—I wanted to wear a tuxedo and work the door. I wasn't sure what I should do, but then fate intervened.

Julie was working the door that night with a guy named Pete. This Pete was a nice enough guy, but he couldn't fight a lick. Sure enough, a fight broke out in the line. Julie was six-one, and the guy he had to deal with was even bigger. Julie could handle himself and so could the other guy. I went over to give Julie a hand, and actually had to jump to hit the guy in the face. He went down and I got him in a headlock.

In order to take him outside, I had to get him through three doors. As we went along, his head served as a battering ram at each door. When we finally got outside, there were three or four steps down to the street. We tripped on the steps and both of us stumbled out to the curb. Just then, a cab pulled up and we both ran into the cab's door. The other guy was just about knocked out.

The door to the cab opened and a very small man got out, the longest cigarette holder I'd ever seen clenched between his teeth. He kind of hissed at me, in a voice I'll never forget, "Get back inside." I did as he said and didn't ask any questions.

I learned later the man was Anthony Carfano, known as "Little Augie Paisano." He was an associate of Lucky Luciano and a victim of a gangland murder on September 25, 1959.

A few minutes after my encounter with Little Augie, I was told Mr. Podell wanted to see me. I went into his office thinking I might get praised for my quick action in ousting the troublemaker. Instead, he lit into me, read me the riot act, and then told me to go back to work.

I went downstairs to the locker room, turned in my waiter's jacket and ID badge, and started walking home. Julie caught up with me and said Mr. Podell wanted to see me again. "I'm not going back. I'm not a waiter and I'm not going to let anybody talk to me the way he did."

"But I think he wants to put you in a tux," Julie said.

I went back.

"You've got a tux," Mr. Podell said. "You start tomorrow night."

So there I was, the day after walking off the job, wearing a tux at the Copa and living the dream.

I was "Joey from the Copa." People would call me looking for a table (if they didn't want to wait in line) or other favors. It was really cool, and I have many memories—most of them fond.

4 : SAMMY DAVIS

In January 1957, the Copa booked Frank Sinatra to do two shows each night for fourteen consecutive nights. All the other acts at the Copa did three shows a night, but because Frank Sinatra was Frank Sinatra, he was able to get his deal for only two shows nightly.

On January 14th, during Sinatra's run, Humphrey Bogart died in Los Angeles. Sinatra and Bogie were friends (there were even rumors that Sinatra had an affair with Bogie's wife, Lauren Bacall) so Old Blue Eyes needed to take a day off and go to California to pay his respects. His two shows for that day had to be covered.

Jerry Lewis was brought in to do the first show and was a total flop. The customers came expecting to see Sinatra and weren't happy to get Lewis instead. There were arguments and fist fights—total chaos. In fact, there were more fights in the place during that one show than there were in all the shows Sinatra did himself.

It happened that Sammy Davis Jr. was in town appearing on Broadway in *Mr. Wonderful* and we were able to get him for the second show. He was fantastic and the crowd loved him. Mr. Podell booked Sammy to do a regular gig. Sammy had previously done his nightclub appearances as part of the Will Mastin Trio. Now, for the first time, he would be the headliner, solo. That's when my friendship with him began and it continued over the years.

Sammy took a room in the Hotel Fourteen at 14 East 60th Street, which was next to and above the Copa. Mr. Podell had a private entrance built to the hotel and many of the headliners took rooms there. In addition to the stars and celebrities, other people with clout were aware of the secret entrance and used it. There was always a line waiting to get in the Copa's main entrance, and these weren't the kind of people who waited in line.

Anyway, I remember that Sinatra returned from California for his next show and Sammy stopped in to see it. At that time, he wore his hair slicked down with pomade. He was wearing a hat that night and when he walked in, he tossed the hat to me. It slipped right through my fingers and onto the floor. I said, "Hey, Sammy. You forgot to change the oil." He got a big kick out of that and laughed like hell.

On most days, I'd stop by his room before work and we'd talk. He loved Western movies and TV shows and had a brown gun belt and holster with a replica gun in it. For his opening act, he got a new black, two-holster gun belt with fake pistols and gave me his old one. Sometimes we'd put our gun belts on and draw on each other. We got to be close friends.

In those days, it wasn't thought to be appropriate for a black man to be with a white woman, and Sammy liked to date white women. When we went out together, we'd have a black woman and a white woman with us. For the sake of appearances, we'd make it look like the white woman was my date, but she was actually there for Sammy.

There were people, some of them pretty powerful, who got really upset over Sammy's penchant for white girls and it caused him problems on occasion. After we'd been friends for a while and he was doing a gig at the Copa, I came into work one day and was told Sammy had been calling for me and wanted to see me right away. I changed into my tux and then went up to his room. I wasn't sure if he was scared or just nervous, but it was obvious to me that something had upset him.

"I got a visit from a couple of guys," he said. "They told me if I don't want to lose my other eye (he lost his left eye in a 1954 car accident), I'd better stop seeing Kim (Novak). What should I do?"

The story circulating at the time was that Harry Cohn, the head of Columbia Pictures where Novak was under contract, was unhappy with the relationship that had developed between his blonde star and Sammy, and wanted it to end. Based on that, I figured the threat had to be taken seriously and I gave it to him straight. "Do you want to lose your other eye?"

"No, of course not."

"Okay, there's your answer."

When I left him that day, he was sitting on the edge of his bed looking very despondent. I felt sorry for him. He was a real pro though, and put on three great shows that night.

Although he wasn't seen with Novak again, he never lost his desire to date white women.

* * *

After the Novak thing, Sammy opened up to me even more. He told me about the racial prejudice he experienced while he was in the military, where he was verbally abused and suffered actual physical beatings. Sammy said that his life was probably saved when a white sergeant came to his defense and the beatings stopped.

His story really hit home with me because I'd been there and done that. What happened to him in 1942 had happened to me in 1949.

The discrimination continued into his entertainment career. Blacks were allowed to entertain white people, but couldn't stay at the same hotels, drink at the same bars, or ride in the same railroad cars.

This time, another white guy intervened. Sammy attributed Frank Sinatra with helping him and all black entertainers to break the color barrier, eventually allowing them to openly mingle with their white fans, stay at the same accommodations, and travel in the same manner.

Another thing that bothered Sammy was the election of John F. Kennedy as president. Sinatra was a big supporter of Kennedy and convinced his entertainer buddies—including Sammy—to back him as well, and they did. After Kennedy won in a squeaker, Sammy thought he might get invited to the inauguration. He didn't.

He blamed the snub on his marriage to white Swedish actress May Britt, at a time when thirty-one states had laws banning interracial marriage.

Kennedy turned out to be an equal opportunity snubber, however. He had promised to visit Sinatra's compound in Palm Springs, but instead went to Bing Crosby's place. Sammy felt Sinatra's known ties to Chicago Outfit boss Sam Giancana made Crosby a safer choice for the new president.

* * *

A couple of final thoughts on Sammy. His father was black and his mother was Puerto Rican. I'll never forget the joke I heard him tell on the stage at the Copa.

"I'm the only black, Puerto Rican, one-eyed Jew in show business."

The other joke he told that brought down the house was what he wrote on a card he sent to Milton Berle.

"Roses are red, violets are blue. I used to be colored, but now I'm a Jew."

I loved you, Sammy. Rest in peace.

5 : SINATRA

Frank Sinatra was again scheduled to headline at the Copa starting the last week in December 1957, but he happened to be in town in early May and stopped in with some friends, had a few drinks, and ate some Chinese food. Mr. Podell personally made sure everything ran smoothly for Sinatra and his party.

When Sinatra had to go to the men's room, Mr. Podell told me to check the restroom to make sure nobody was in there who might annoy the star while he was using the facilities. I saw to it the room was empty and stood outside the door until Sinatra came out. He thanked me and I walked him back to his table.

Sinatra didn't have to pay for anything, of course—Mr. Podell picked up the tab. He was a good tipper though, and gave the staff a hundred bucks each. In fact, when word got out that Sinatra was in the house, several of the waiters from downstairs came up to get in on the tips, although they had nothing to do with serving his party. After finishing their meal, I escorted them down to the showroom to catch the last show.

One of the guys who worked for Sinatra came over and offered me a C-note ($100). I said, "What the hell is this for? I didn't do anything."

"Frank wanted you to have it," he said. That's the way Sinatra operated.

* * *

When Sinatra opened that winter, it was wall-to-wall excitement. It was bitterly cold, but people stood in line for an hour or more to get inside. And anyone working the door had all kinds of money thrown at them by people wanting to cut the line. We couldn't accept the bribes though, because Mr. Podell issued an order that nobody would get preferential treatment—everybody had to wait their turn.

However, we were able to work around that order for some of our regular customers. We'd allow them into the lounge and not the showroom and not accept a tip. Some of the regulars knew the back way from the lounge to the showroom and took it downstairs, where they'd duke (tip) Ronnie the maître d' real good and he'd take care of them. Other than that, nobody bought their way into the showroom.

Some people tried to use their connections rather than money to jump the line. There was one lady who was married to a very wealthy man and had met Mr. Podell in the past. She said to me, "Tell Julie (Mr. Podell) I'm in line and I'm not going to wait." I told her to give me a few minutes and I'd talk to Mr. Podell. When I got inside, I told him about the woman and delivered her message. He looked me in the eye and in that gruff New York voice of his said, "Tell her to go fuck herself." I didn't tell her that, of course. When I went back outside, and she confronted me, I told her Mr. Podell was so busy I hadn't been able to talk with him.

Because Sinatra was drawing such large crowds, Mr. Podell put on a couple of extra guys to help out. One of them was a huge guy named Lenny Montana. Fifteen years later, he played Luca Brasi in *The Godfather*.

Lenny was outside and I was inside the door, directing people to the showroom. Suddenly, a guy tapped me on the shoulder and said, "Can you show me to the ballroom?"

Ballroom? I almost laughed in his face. I said, "We don't have a ballroom. We only have a showroom."

"Well, I gave the man outside a hundred bucks and he said to come in and you'd get me into the show."

"Look, pal, I don't know what the guy outside told you, but you can't come in. Go back outside and tell him that."

He went out and a few seconds later, Lenny came in. He said, "Joe, you've gotta let this guy in."

I knew Lenny could twist me up like a pretzel, but I said, "Listen to me. The boss said nobody cuts the line. I don't want any trouble with him and I don't want any trouble with you. But as long as I'm on the fucking door, *nobody* gets in. If you send them in a different way, I've got no problem with it. If I'm gone on break and you let somebody in, I've got no problem with it. But while I'm here, *nobody* gets in. Understand?"

Lenny went back outside and that was the end of it.

* * *

I'm not sure what the seating capacity for the showroom was at that time, but I think it was 670. But we were packing at least 1,000 people in there for every show. Every seat at the tables was full and people were standing in every nook and cranny.

Pauly and I had to walk Sinatra on and off the showroom floor for each performance, which with those crowds was no easy task. You could feel the electricity in the air that his mere presence generated—it was unreal. We'd clasp our hands over his head as we walked him into the room, and one time, a guy reached in and grabbed Sinatra's handkerchief. Sinatra blew his stack and wanted to go after the guy and get his handkerchief back, but we forced him out onto the floor.

When Sinatra started his shows, he immediately captivated his audience. I've never seen anything like it before or since. He'd sing "Birth of the Blues" and the crowd would be on its feet yelling and screaming. He'd follow that with a song like "With Every Breath I Take" and you could hear a pin drop. He was able to quiet the crowds down without saying a word, just by singing. It was amazing.

While Sinatra was performing, there was no food or alcohol service; you could only get a drink if you had purchased a bottle and had it on the table. If he was singing a ballad, the room would be totally silent, and if someone put an ice cube in their glass, the noise would cause them to get nasty looks from anyone around them.

I remember once when Sinatra was singing, I saw a guy with his head on the table, pounding the tabletop with his hand. I walked over and lifted his head up. "Are you okay?" I asked. He said, "Yeah, I'm alright. I just wish I was a broad, so I could scream." That was how Sinatra affected his audiences. His fans adored him.

On the closing night of Sinatra's show, ten or twelve of his mobster friends from Chicago flew in. After his last performance, they all came up to the lounge, and Sinatra and Mr. Podell joined them. They'd all been drinking for hours and none of them were feeling any pain. One of the guys told Mr. Podell he wanted a photo of everybody, so Mr. Podell ordered twelve pictures. I told the camera girl,

"Mr. Podell wants twelve pictures, but take thirteen because I want one too."

She took the thirteen pictures, but instead of giving one to me, she handed them all to Mr. Podell. He handed them out to everybody and had one left over. He said to the girl, "What's this?"

"That's for Joey. He wanted one."

Mr. Podell turned to me. "Is that true, Joey? You wanted this picture?"

What could I say? "Yeah, boss, I want the picture."

To my surprise, Mr. Podell took the photo and wrote on it, "To my boy Joey." Then Sinatra said, "Me too" and grabbed the picture and signed it. I couldn't believe it! I was thrilled but I had an even bigger surprise coming.

I was standing by the door when Frank's go-to guy (I think his name was Tony) came up to me. "Frank wants you to go to work for him," he said.

I didn't know what to say and I think I stuttered when I said, "I can't."

"Why?"

I said stupidly, "Because I don't have any suits and my wife just gave birth to my son."

He said, "That's okay. Frank will buy you all the suits you want."

I said, "Really, thanks but no thanks. I can't accept."

The reason I declined was that as I regained my composure, I remembered stories I'd heard that when Sinatra got drunk, he sometimes abused his people. He'd order them around and make them get his shoes and underwear for him. I knew if he told me to get his underwear, I'd tell him to go fuck himself. Still, I sometimes wonder if turning down that offer might have been the biggest mistake of my life.

6 : BASEBRAWL

On May 16, 1957, an incident took place at the Copa that was of major interest in New York City and the sports world. It involved a fight between several New York Yankees baseball players and a group of bowlers. The Yankees players were out celebrating second baseman Billy Martin's twenty-ninth birthday. The bowlers were there partying after attending a bowling tournament. As you can imagine, the fracas received wide media coverage.

Although there were some variations, the reports were generally in agreement that Mickey Mantle, Yogi Berra, Whitey Ford, Hank Bauer, Johnny Kucks, their wives, and Billy Martin had been out on the town. After finishing a late dinner at Danny's Hideaway, they decided to go to the Copa to catch Sammy Davis, who was headlining there at the time. The players frequented the Copa and were fans of Sammy's, so that decision was nothing out of the ordinary.

Unfortunately, the bowlers were there as well, and many of them already had a bit too much to drink. When Sammy came on stage, some of the bowlers started heckling him with racial slurs and using colorful language. One of the Yankees, possibly Martin, asked the bowlers to watch their language and let Sammy do his show. Words were exchanged and someone suggested the matter be settled outside. But it didn't get that far before punches were thrown.

One of the bowlers—a Bronx deli owner—suffered a broken nose and jaw. One account said he was knocked out cold on the floor of the cloak room. Another said he was unconscious on the floor of the men's room. But there was no disagreement on the nature of the injuries. The injured man filed a criminal complaint naming Hank Bauer as his assailant, resulting in a grand jury hearing evidence.

Mickey Mantle was not used to being in a courtroom setting, and when he was called to testify, he was understandably nervous at first. He was chewing gum when he was sworn in and wanted to get rid of it, but didn't know where. He solved the problem by sticking the wad of gum under his chair.

A grand juror asked him, "Well, did you see a gentleman lying unconscious on the floor near the Copa entrance?"

"Yes, I did," Mantle answered.

"All right. Do you have an opinion as to how this could have happened?"

Mantle thought about the question and then, with a serious look on his face, said "I think Roy Rogers rode through the Copa, and Trigger kicked the man in the head."

The jurors broke out laughing, and an hour later, the district attorney threw out the case for insufficient evidence.

Subsequently, the Yankees fined Mantle, Berra, Ford, Bauer, and Martin a thousand dollars each for their conduct. Kucks was penalized seven hundred. And a month later, Yankees general manager George Weiss traded the fiery Martin to the Kansas City Athletics. Weiss thought Martin was a bad influence on Mantle, and had been looking for a reason to get rid of him. The Copa event served that purpose.

Those accounts were primarily accurate, but not entirely.

* * *

I was at the Copa the night of the fight, not working, but as a customer. Because employees weren't allowed to be in the place while off duty, I wasn't in a position to make any statements to the media or anyone else about what happened. And I had no reason to say anything about it until now. But I was both a witness and a participant that night, so I'm going to take this opportunity to clarify a couple of things.

First, let me say that what was reported by the media was primarily accurate. The Yankees players did stop at the Copa regularly and I knew them personally. Sammy Davis was performing, the bowlers were there, and some of them were drunk and obnoxious.

I violated Copa policy by going to the club to catch Sammy's show. I was willing to take that chance because Sammy told me the day before (Tuesday) that he planned to do his gun routine the next night. He was very good at handling those pistols and I really wanted to see him in action in front of an audience.

I said, "Sammy, I'd love to, but I'm off on Wednesdays."

He said, "Joe, you've gotta come and see me do my thing."

The only way an employee could be in the club on their day off was with Mr. Podell's permission. Violating that policy was grounds for dismissal. But to my knowledge, he never approved such a request. I knew Mr. Podell liked me, so I decided not to ask him and to just show up and take my chances. If I got caught, I'd have to hope he'd cut me some slack.

Wearing a brown suit, I entered the club Wednesday night using the service entrance. That allowed me to bypass

Mr. Podell's regular table. Of course, I still had to be concerned he'd spot me during one of his walks around or one of his snitches would squeal on me. Murray, the lounge manager and a standup guy, arranged for me to sit at a table at ringside (close to the stage, but out of Mr. Podell's line of vision) with Harry Belafonte and Sidney Poitier and their wives, and Sy Devore, who made all the costumes for the Copa Girls.

It must have been around 10 or 10:30 when Murray came to the table and told me that Mickey, Whitey, Yogi, Johnny, Hank, their wives, and Billy Martin had just come in. They didn't seem to be feeling any pain and were asking for me.

I'd become good friends with Mickey and Billy. I always took good care of them when they came to the Copa. And sometimes they'd call me from other joints (they really liked Danny's Hideaway and Ed Wynn's Harwin Club) and invite me to stop for a drink with them when I got off. Under the circumstances, I asked Murray to tell them I had the night off. But he told them I was there anyway. The Yankees group ended up getting a table on the other side of the room.

Just before Sammy came on, the group of bowlers came in. They'd won some kind of championship and were out celebrating. Some of them were loud and acted like they were already intoxicated. They happened to get seated at a table next to Mickey, Billy, and the others. Not a good situation. Murray came by to tell me he thought there was going to be a problem.

Sammy came on and began singing and dancing up a storm. He was famous for doing impersonations of stars like Jimmy Stewart, Frank Sinatra, Jimmy Cagney, and others. In my opinion, Rich Little was the only impersonator better than Sammy.

But Sammy was multi-talented—he not only sang and danced, he also played trumpet and drums—and liked to showcase his other abilities.

The bowlers weren't happy and started yelling racial stuff at him, like calling him Black Sambo, using profanity, and demanding he do his impersonations.

Hank Bauer, who like me was wearing a brown suit, asked them nicely to tone it down so everyone could enjoy the show. They paid no attention to him. Pauly, my regular partner, tried to make peace between the two tables, but he was wasting his breath.

A few minutes later, Billy went to the bowlers' table and asked them again to cool it. Words were exchanged and one of the bowlers offered to go outside to settle the matter. Billy being Billy didn't need to be invited twice and started for the door, the bowlers following behind him. Mickey then joined the group going out to fight.

Murray came to me again and said, "Pauly's got a problem." I had no choice but to give him a hand, even if Mr. Podell saw me and it cost me my job.

As I got to the other side of the club, I saw Hank walking around, apparently looking for Billy and Mickey. I grabbed him and sat him in a chair. I said, "I know where Mickey and Billy went. Stay here, and I'll get them and bring them back to you."

I started for the stairs to the service entrance where I'd seen everybody go. When I got there, the noise was overwhelming, with a lot of shouting and cursing. I was the last guy in line behind the bowlers. I pushed the guy in front of me forward into the guy in front of him, like dominoes. Then I saw Pauly in the stairway in a confrontation with one of the bowlers. He was a great big guy and if he hit Pauly, he could have hurt him bad.

My momentum was taking me right past the guy. I hit him with a left and then a right. His blood spurted all over me and he dropped to the floor, out cold. It turned out I broke his jaw and nose. Just then, somebody jumped on my back: it was Billy Martin—he didn't recognize me without my tux and thought I was one of the bowlers. We both fell to the floor, then he realized who I was. Pauly picked both of us up and that was the end of the fight.

Then it was time for me to get out of there. I told Pauly I was going to go up to Sammy's hotel room (his door was never locked) until things calmed down. I asked him to call me when it was safe. After what seemed like an eternity, the phone rang. But it wasn't Pauly; it was Mickey. He'd been asking for me and Pauly told him where I was.

Mickey said, "Joey, we just had a big fight. Oh my God, what a fight. You should have seen it."

As far as I know, Mickey wasn't involved in the fisticuffs. He might have seen the guy I knocked out on the floor, though, because when asked by the grand jury, he said, "I think Roy Rogers rode through the Copa, and Trigger kicked the man in the head."

I waited another half hour, then snuck out of the hotel and caught the subway home. After taking the risk, I didn't even get to see Sammy's gun routine.

The next day, all the papers reported on the "brawl." And Hank Bauer—the other guy in a brown suit—was named as the jaw breaker.

I went to work that night with trepidation, not knowing what to expect. I went to the lounge looking for Murray. He wasn't there, but somebody else was. A good friend of Mr. Podell, a very important man, said, "I want to talk to you."

"Sure."

"Were you here last night?"

I hesitated briefly, then said, "I don't work on Wednesday nights."

"That's not what I asked you."

I had no intention of snitching on myself. "No. I wasn't here."

As I was changing into my tux, it came to me why he'd asked if I'd been in the club during the fight. He wasn't just fishing; he knew. The guy was playing around with the cigarette girl and I knew she'd seen me. Oops.

A little before we opened at six o'clock, the phone rang. "Copa Lounge, Joey."

It was Mr. Podell. "Joey, I want you in my office. *Now*."

When I entered his office, his friend who had questioned me earlier and Murray were there with him. Things didn't look good and I was expecting the worst. "Joey," he said, "were you here last night?"

I played the same game I tried on Podell's buddy earlier. "Mr. Podell, I don't work on Wednesdays."

"Okay, Joey. That's all."

I walked out of that room in disbelief and never heard another word about it. In addition to getting off the hook, a grand jury declined to indict the innocent Hank Bauer for assaulting the bowler. This is a story that truly had a happy ending.

7 : OTHER STORIES FROM THE COPA

DEAN & JERRY

I want to talk about the last time Dean Martin and Jerry Lewis worked at the Copa, on July 25, 1956. That was where they did their last show as a team.

In my opinion, Jerry wasn't an especially nice guy. However, Dean Martin was one of the grooviest guys I ever met. He was good looking, loved the broads, and they loved him.

There were three bars in the Copa. Two of them were in the lounge. One had barstools where customers could sit and drink. The other was a service bar in the back of the room that handled orders for the tables. The third, a large service bar, was located in the kitchen and took care of the showroom. I want to mention here that it was Mr. Podell's policy that whenever a customer asked for a specific brand name, that's what they got—never a well drink.

On this particular night, the bartender assigned to the bar in the kitchen took sick and had to go home. I was sent down to replace him and work with the head bartender. When I got behind the bar, the head bartender was serving drinks to Mr. Podell, Jerry Lewis, and former baseball player and manager

Leo Durocher, who was temporarily out of baseball. Dean Martin came in, walked by them without a word, and stopped right in front of me. He picked up a clean cocktail glass, turned it right side up, and said, "Cutty Sark, Goombah. I'll say when." I filled the glass to the top. He took it from me, raised it, and said, "*Salud*." Then he downed the whole drink in one gulp. So when you hear that Dean faked it on his TV show, don't believe it—he drank. After finishing the drink, he walked out, again without acknowledging Mr. Podell, Leo, or Jerry.

It was obvious to me that there was no love lost between Dean and Jerry. It was no surprise this was their final appearance together.

I've got to say that as charismatic as Frank Sinatra was with his voice and charm, I think Dean was even more so. As far as I'm concerned, he had it all and was a complete entertainer. He would walk over to a table while singing, pick up a drink glass usually belonging to a good-looking woman (the *maître d'* was responsible for putting good-looking people in the front row), lower his voice and say, "Are you gonna sit there and tell me you don't love me?" The woman and the audience loved it.

I doubt if there will ever be another like him.

* * *

CONNECTIONS

At the Copa, we had many, many fights. That was the nature of the business. At that time, Tammany Hall (the powerful political organization) was headed by Carmine DeSapio. He was known as the political kingmaker, and although there were stories he was associated with mobster Frank Costello, they didn't interfere with his rise to power.

Mr. Podell always made sure these kinds of people were taken care of at the Copa, because they then took care of him. In spite of all the fights we had, I only got pinched once and came close another time.

The close call had to do with a fight outside involving four people—two men and two women. I was fighting with one of the guys and my partner Pauly was battling the other one, when one of the women hit me in the head with her huge pocketbook. It contained drink glasses and an ashtray she'd taken from the Copa as souvenirs. She really belted me, but I couldn't hit a woman, so I kept punching the guy. When he went down, somebody grabbed me from behind. I swung around and hit him, and down he went too. Unfortunately, it was a cop.

After the fight broke up, I was called into Mr. Podell's office and several cops were in there too. He asked me if I knew the guy was a cop when I hit him. I told the truth. I didn't know. I was told I could leave and that was the end of it.

The time I got arrested and had to go to court involved a huge brawl, and some of the customers involved claimed to have been hurt. They identified me as the guy who caused their injuries.

Mr. Podell told me that when I went to court, they'd ask me my job title. We didn't have job titles, so he told me to say I was a supervisor. From that time on, Pauly and I were supervisors.

When I went to court, the case got dismissed. No fine or jail time—nothing.

It had been a serious incident though, and prompted me to come up with a saying: "Whenever you have lots of booze and broads, you're going to have brawls."

* * *

BUDD SCHULBERG

One night, screenwriter, sports writer, and novelist Budd Schulberg came into the lounge and sat at the bar. He was a real nice man, and was always cordial to me. After a while, the bartender called me over and nodded to where Schulberg was seated. He said, "Those two guys are busting Budd's balls pretty bad. There might be trouble."

I wanted to get Budd away from the bar so I walked over to him and said, "Excuse me, Mr. Schulberg, you have a phone call."

After he walked away, I said to the troublemakers, "Pay your check, you're leaving."

One of them said, real surly, "We aren't finished with our drinks yet."

I knocked his glass over. "You're finished now."

He started to throw a punch but I beat him to it. I hit him with a right and he went down and out. His buddy sat there and didn't say a word. By the time Budd got back from the phantom phone call, everything was over, and his two antagonists were gone.

It happened that filming was underway for his first movie, *A Face in the Crowd*, starring Andy Griffith. He offered me a walk-on part. I turned down the offer. He later offered me a walk-on in another movie, *Wind Across the Everglades*. I politely turned him down again. I guess I was just never star struck.

* * *

HITTING THE WRONG GUY

For Frank Sinatra's show in 1958, Mr. Podell wanted all the stools removed from the bar in the lounge. The manager assigned me to make sure they were moved to the service bar. I told Pete, the other doorman, to get some busboys to get the stools out of there and he could supervise them.

I was able to see the bar from my spot at the door and the job was getting done. When I looked again, one of the other employees was carrying the stools back out. Pete was just standing there, watching. I ran over and asked the guy carrying the stools what he was doing.

"I don't want them back there. I want them out here," he said.

"You do? Who in the fuck are *you* to decide that? They're being taken back there on Mr. Podell's orders."

The guy didn't want to listen and one word led to another. Pretty soon, I hit him—another broken jaw.

When I told Pauly about it, he said, "Oh my god, Joey. That guy's Tony G.'s son-in-law."

Tony G. was a very powerful person with organized crime connections.

That night my friend Sal came in. He asked me if I knew the identity of the guy I punched. My first answer was "Yes." He asked me again and this time I got the message. I said, "No."

The following night, Sal and Tony G. came in and had a conversation at one of the tables. Then they called me over. Tony G. asked me, "Did you know the man you hit yesterday was my son-in-law?"

"No."

"He didn't tell you who his father-in-law is?"

"No."

"Okay. Go back to what you were doing."

That was it—case closed. I didn't get in any trouble. This was the first time Sal bailed me out, but it wasn't the last.

* * *

PICKING UP DIMES

Pearl Bailey was performing her second show of the night. During the first show, she had received a note stating that she'd "pay for strutting your black ass around." Pearl was a tremendous entertainer and did the second show in spite of the threat.

Errol Flynn came in and he had a pretty good package on. He got a table just off ringside and he and Pearl had a great banter going that turned a bit risqué. Pearl told Errol that when she started in the entertainment business, it was customary for white customers to tip black female performers by turning their glass upside down on their table and placing a silver dollar on top of it. The black girls would then have to go to the table, hike up their dress, and pick the coin up using their vagina.

She said some of the customers weren't very nice guys. They would heat the coins with their lighters, and she had the scars to prove it. Not everyone in the audience understood what she was talking about, but Errol did and he thought the story was hilarious. He really cracked up, though, when Pearl said she got so good at it, she was eventually able to pick up dimes.

I knew what she was saying too, because my cousin and I used to hang out at a black club called The Savannah in Greenwich Village. The most beautiful mixed race girls worked there and were called "high yellows." They also told their audiences about picking up tips the same way.

* * *

THE NOTE

I really had a good time working at the Copa. Some nights were very exciting, and others were more normal, depending on who was appearing. When Sinatra was there, it was always exciting. What I'm going to tell you next turned out alright, but it could have been a real disaster for me.

Sinatra was appearing, it was his second show, and I was working the door. A Jewish guy, who was a bigshot in the garment district, came in with a gorgeous lady. Sometimes women would flirt with me, and while he was checking his coat, she and I made eye contact but nothing was said.

After the show broke, they came up the stairs and she was a few steps ahead of her date. When he went to get his coat, she slipped a piece of paper into my hand. Unfortunately, the guy saw her move and came right over to me.

"Give me that note," he said.

I knew her phone number was probably on the piece of paper and there would be big trouble if I gave it up.

When I didn't respond, he became furious. He turned to Pauly and said loudly, "Get Murray! Get Murray!"

While he was engaged with Pauly, I threw the piece of paper behind a sand-filled canister used to dispose of cigarettes that was located next to me.

When Murray came over, the guy said, "I want to see Julie (Mr. Podell). Have him come over here right now."

Murray ran like a scared rabbit and returned with Mr. Podell. The guy shouted, "She handed him a piece of paper! I want to know what it said."

Mr. Podell told him to calm down and then said to me, "Joey, do you have a piece of paper the lady gave you?"

"No, boss, I don't have any paper."

The guy hollered, "She gave it to him, I saw it. It's in his hand."

Mr. Podell asked, "What have you got in your hand, Joey?"

I opened my palm and handed Mr. Podell a book of matches. He gave it to the irate guy. He opened it up and of course there was nothing written in it. He said, "But I saw her hand him something."

Mr. Podell said, "Well, as you saw, he had nothing in his hand but the matches."

The guy made a final effort to save face. "What's he got those matches in his hand for anyway?"

"*All* my people carry them in case someone needs a light."

That was it. After the guy and the lady left, Mr. Podell said, "Joey, did she give you anything?"

I hated to lie to him, but I said, "No, boss. I just had the matches like I always do."

WHEN WIFE MEETS GIRLFRIEND

On another night, a very powerful VIP type—a really tough and mean guy, Mr. Green—came in with his girlfriend and went to the bar. None of us liked him or wanted anything to do with him, so we never escorted him to the bar or a table.

About a half hour later, a woman came to the door and asked for Mr. Green. It was policy that when an unescorted woman asked for someone by name, an employee had to personally walk her to the party she wished to see. The lady was brought to the bar where Mr. Green and his girlfriend were. Unbeknownst to me or any of the other guys, the new arrival was Mr. Green's wife.

I said Mr. Green was tough, and so was his wife. She hit her husband's girlfriend in the jaw and knocked her right on her ass, then walked out.

Mr. Green didn't seem to know what he should do. After a brief hesitation, he picked his girlfriend up from the floor and walked her out the rear exit, but we were pretty sure he'd be back and wouldn't be happy. To be safe, Murray told the doorman who had escorted Mr. Green's wife to the bar to get off the floor and go home. I replaced him on the door.

That was fine, but I bore a resemblance to the doorman. I told Murray, "When Mr. Green comes back and sees me, he might think I'm the guy who brought his wife in, and start throwing punches. No fucking way am I gonna play punching bag for him. If he hits me, I'll hit him right back." Murray got flustered and started stuttering. I said, "I'll tell you what, you stand at the door. Green knows who you are and he won't take any shots at you. I'm going home."

When I came back to work the next day everything was cool and there hadn't been any problems. But from then on, whenever Mr. Green came in, I kept away from him and we never had a problem.

* * *

Although I really enjoyed working at the Copa, eventually the thrill of it all faded, and it became time for me to move on. When I told Mr. Podell I was leaving, he blew his top. He asked if I wanted to go back working behind the bar or on the floor as a captain. I said it wasn't that I was looking for a better position. It was time for me to leave and I gave him my two weeks' notice. When I left, he didn't even say goodbye to me.

8 : THE HEALTH CLUB

After leaving the Copa, I knocked around for a while, moving from job to job. It was in the mid-60s. I was thirty-four years old and played a lot of touch football, baseball, worked out with weights, and punched the heavy bag regularly—I was in great shape.

I was working at a gas station one day when a big black Cadillac pulled up. The window rolled down and the driver said, "Fill it up, please."

As I was pumping the gas, the driver got out of the car. He said, "You look like you take good care of yourself. Do you belong to a health club?"

"No, but I play a lot of sports and go to the gym when I can."

"How'd you like to work at a health club as an instructor?"

I wasn't real happy with pumping gas and I was into fitness. "Why not?" I said.

He gave me his card. His name was Bernie Broome, a lawyer for the Shelton Health Club, located in the Shelton Hotel (now the Marriott East Side Hotel) at 525 Lexington Avenue. They had a total of five clubs, one in each borough. We made an appointment for me to see him at the Forest Hills, Queens, location—called The Spa—on my day off.

On the day of the meeting, two co-owners of the club were there as well. They were both in their twenties and very nice guys. The interview went smoothly and I was offered a job as a gym instructor.

I loved the job right from the start. I got along well with other staff, and helping people in their workouts was right up my alley. What I didn't know was that I wasn't going to stay in Queens. Management had other plans for me.

After a few months on the job, Bernie took me into the city and showed me the Manhattan club. It was absolutely magnificent. On the drive back to Queens, Bernie asked if I'd thought about working in the city. I assumed he meant as an assistant to the instructor running the gym.

And then he said, "I'd like you to work in Manhattan as a salesperson, selling memberships."

I was skeptical. "I've never sold anything in my life."

"Don't worry about that. With your personality and appearance, you'll do just fine."

"Okay. I'll give it a try."

Bernie was right. I wound up becoming the number one salesman in New York City and managed the club in Manhattan.

* * *

I was only at the Manhattan location about six months before being promoted to manager. Almost as soon as I took the position, I hired a couple of sharp salesmen who did really well for themselves and the club.

The existing staff accepted me in my new role, except for one. The locker room attendant didn't want me to interfere in his domain. He made sure the members had everything they wanted. They loved him for it and he made a lot of money. However, after he got to know me and realized I wasn't going to infringe on his operation, we got along very well.

My closest friend there, though, was Frank Zappella. We had initially met when I worked at the club in Queens. Frank took care of the pools and maintenance at all five clubs. He also did some selling, but didn't like it and preferred to do maintenance work. When it came to that, there was almost nothing he couldn't do.

I thought of Frank as my Cheyenne Bodie (played by actor Clint Walker in the TV series *Cheyenne*). Frank stood six feet tall and weighed around two hundred-fifteen pounds—without an ounce of fat. He was a legitimate tough guy and never used anything but his hands when there was trouble. He was known all over town, and everybody who knew him respected him. He was smart too—just a terrific guy.

There was a bar on 53rd Street and Third Avenue named P.J. Clarke's, where a lot of ballplayers and other sports celebrities hung out when they were in town. I remember when the New York Giants were hosting a team from out west, several of the visiting players were in the bar, and so were Frank and I.

A guy Frank knew got into a beef with one of the players. Frank intervened and calmed things down before the guy got his ass kicked. As the night wore on and his friend had more to drink, he got into an argument with a huge lineman and got right in his face. Frank again intervened.

This time, though, the lineman got an attitude toward Frank. They were talking things over when another player came over and threw a punch at Frank. Frank decked the guy—knocked him out cold. The lineman he'd been arguing with didn't say a word, but boxer Jake LaMotta, aka the Raging Bull, was there, and *he* did. "You shouldn't have hit that guy. He was just sticking up for his friend."

Frank Didn't like LaMotta at all, and told him, "You can go fuck yourself. And if you don't get out of here, I'm going to hit you right between the eyes."

LaMotta *ran* out of the place without another word.

Frank was also a great swimmer. One day we were having a cup of coffee in the locker room, which was next to the pool, when one of the members came in and said there was a young guy at the pool who was kind of a loudmouth. He was bragging he'd bet a hundred bucks that he could swim the backstroke two lengths of the pool before anyone else could do it freestyle.

I went out to the pool and he challenged me to that bet. I told him I wasn't interested, but knew somebody who might be. I went into the locker room and came back with Frank. He told the guy, "I really don't want to take advantage of you."

The kid sneered at him. "Don't worry about that. This will be the easiest hundred I ever made."

The big mouth and I each put up a hundred dollars and gave it to the locker room attendant to hold. Then he and Frank got into the pool. Frank completed his two laps before the kid finished one. Frank and I split the winnings.

Frank passed away over twenty years ago and his wife never remarried. She once said to me, "Joe, where would I ever find another Frank?"

I couldn't agree more.

* * *

In Manhattan, the men's club was in the basement and its Olympic-size swimming pool was in the sub-basement. This was the same pool in which Buster Crabbe trained for his 1932 gold medal-winning Olympic performance.

The women's club was on the sixteenth floor. They had the same facilities as the men, except the pool. The ladies had to come down to the men's club if they wanted to swim. I mention the ladies because there were a number of very attractive women who were members. Actress Ali McGraw used the club's pool to prepare for a scene in the hit movie *Love Story*.

One morning when I arrived for work at around eleven, I saw the entrance to the club was filled with cables and wires leading into the locker room. I asked the receptionist what was going on. She said she had booked a film crew shooting a movie starring George Segal to use the pool from ten that morning until noon. They had agreed to pay the club a five hundred dollar rental fee. She said she hadn't told me because she wanted it to be a surprise.

It was definitely a surprise. Those were peak hours for us and I never would have approved the deal.

I walked into the locker room as the shoot was going on and I heard a guy holler, "Cut! Cut!"

Then he said to me, "You can't come in here! We're shooting a scene."

I asked, "Who's in charge?"

Another guy came over. He said, "Sir, we're shooting a scene. You're going to have to leave."

"Let me explain something to you. This is *my* club. If anybody leaves, it's going to be *you*."

Next the director came over. "We're paying for the use of this facility and we intend to use the time we agreed to."

"What you did was take advantage of my receptionist," I said. "And now you're interfering with my business."

As we were talking, yet another guy walked up and told the director they were ready to shoot the pool scene. This thing was bigger than I'd thought and I was getting more annoyed. The director and I went from the locker room to the pool, where a big camera had been set up.

I said, "Get that camera out of here."

"I can't do that," he said in a pleading voice.

"Either you move it or I'll throw it in the pool." I made a move toward the camera.

"Please, please, can't we work this out?"

Sensing his desperation, I accepted his offer to negotiate. I told him they could have the use of the facility until one o'clock, but it would cost an additional thousand dollars.

"That's too much," he said. "I can't afford it."

"That's the price. Either you pay it or the camera's going in the pool. It's the last time I'm going to tell you."

He paid the extra thousand.

I collected the money—five hundred in cash and a check for the other five—and went out to the reception area. Dick, one of the owners, was there talking to her. She'd told him about the rental deal, but neither of them knew I got the extra thousand. When I turned the cash and check over, Dick was surprised and very happy.

In fact, he was so thrilled he took one of the salesmen and me to Gatsby's, which at the time was one of the most popular bistros in the city.

* * *

Bill, a boyhood friend of mine, was a bookmaker and I arranged for him to get the action at the Copa. Sometimes he'd pick me up and I'd go there with him. While he took care of his business, I'd hang out in the lounge and talk with my former co-workers.

One night, Bill had a girl with him he was dating, who would later become his wife. He explained she wanted to take in the show at the Copa so he brought her along. I didn't know who was playing that night, but I had no problem with her coming with us.

When we got near the Copa, the line of people waiting to get in stretched for blocks. We walked up to the front of the line and I asked the doorman if I could speak to Pauly. When he came out, I asked what was going on to draw that kind of crowd.

He said, "Tom Jones is here."

That explained it. Jones had appeared at the Copa early in his career, before he had a real hit record, and hadn't done that great. Since then he'd been on fire with ten or so hits. For his next appearances, every performance was completely sold out.

I think it's safe to say that Tom Jones drew as well as Frank Sinatra. The downside was while Sinatra attracted adult crowds, Jones was a teenage idol and kids made up a large part of his audience. And the younger patrons were tougher to control.

Anyway, Pauly took us inside and got us a good table. Jones put on a tremendous performance and his fans were going wild.

All of a sudden, Pauly came to our table and said he needed me to come back to work until Jones left town. At first I turned him down, but he kept asking. I finally gave in and said I'd give him a hand.

The problem Pauly was having resulted when some guys claimed they duked (tipped) a seating captain to get a better table. The captain took their money and told them he'd be back to get them as soon as he could arrange for something closer. He never came back and those guys were pissed. Pauly tried to calm them down, but they weren't buying it. That's when the fists started flying. The brawl was as bad as the one with the Yankees players, if not worse.

I was back the next night, in my tux and working the line. Due to the size of the crowds, we had police-type barricades set up for the people to stand behind and give us a little better control. We admitted them based on the word of a seating captain. He'd tell us how many people to let in. When that group had been seated, he'd come back and let us know how many more he was ready for.

It was freezing cold and the people in the line—especially the kids—demanded to be let inside. When told they had to wait their turn, they became verbally abusive.

I went inside for some hot coffee, and when I came back out, moved down to work the center of the line. I saw a middle-aged woman try to cut the line by crawling under the barricade. You had to be very careful about putting your hands on a woman, but I couldn't ignore what she'd done or there would be trouble from the people she cut in front of.

Very gingerly, I put my hand on the top of her head. I told her she couldn't stay there and had to come with me. She complied without a problem, but after we'd gone a few feet, she started calling a man's name. I don't know if he was her husband, boyfriend, or brother, but this guy came over and started arguing with me.

After a few words back and forth, he threw a punch. I slipped his punch and hit him with one of my own, knocking him down. Before he even got back on his feet, he started calling for the cops. I knew I had to get off the line, so I went inside and told the manager what had happened. He told me to go downstairs and cool off. The good thing was I didn't have to go back out in that cold.

Mr. Podell asked me about the incident later that night. He was well in his cups by then, so I just told him I hadn't intended to hit the guy, it was strictly a reflex reaction. He accepted my explanation and that was the end of it.

* * *

In addition to the general chaos surrounding Tom Jones's shows, there were some rather humorous incidents.

We had to walk him on and off the showroom floor with our hands intertwined over his head to prevent fans from grabbing his head or face. During the show, Pauly and I sat on chairs next to the band, behind and to either side of him. Pauly's chair was near the piano and mine was a couple of feet from the trombone player.

I saw a woman get up from her table and crawl toward the piano on her hands and knees. By the time I got Pauly's attention, she was under the piano, between it and the piano player's stool. Pauly couldn't reach her without disrupting the piano player, but her legs were sticking out so he grabbed them, pulled her clear, and sent her back to her table.

Every so often during his shows, Jones would stop at a table and give one of the women a kiss. One of the girls wrapped her arms around his neck, put a lip-lock on him and wouldn't let go. I grabbed him, the woman's date grabbed her, and we were able to pull them apart.

There was a similar incident which was much more personal.

My daughter Linda and her girlfriend came to see Jones. During the show, Jones sometimes invited girls from the audience to come on the stage where he'd give them a kiss. My daughter got up from her seat and walked over to the stairs to the stage where I was standing.

I said, "What's the matter?"

"Nothing. I just want to kiss Tom Jones. Can I?" I hesitated. "Come on, Daddy, can I?"

"I guess so. Go back to your table and I'll give you the signal when to go. Keep an eye on me."

When Jones was ready to start inviting girls to the stage, I nodded to Linda. She was and still is a beautiful girl, and that night she was wearing a really gorgeous outfit. As she walked toward the stage, the audience applauded and a lot of the guys whistled.

You have to remember that Linda was only eighteen, but she was still my baby. I was figuring the kiss would be a little peck on the cheek. Was I wrong!

When she got in front of Jones, he took her in his arms and gave her a full lip-lock.

Jesus Christ! I'd never seen Linda kiss a guy before and I was in shock. I fought back the urge to run over, separate them, and give Jones a crack.

When Linda walked back to her table, she got a standing ovation. I'm sure it was a night she'll never forget. I know I won't.

I stayed on through Jones's run as I had promised Pauly. I was glad when it ended, though. I'd had enough of Tom Jones and the turmoil that came with his shows.

9 : STUEY UNGAR

While working at the health club, I missed the gambling and running poker and crap games. So I began working part time at a nightly poker game run by Jack Pearl. When the club closed, I was able to put in additional hours working for Mr. Pearl. The game was held on the second floor of an apartment building where there was a large room with the poker table, a smaller room used as an office, a small kitchen, and a bathroom. The game was seven-card stud, with two and four-dollar bets, and players could check and raise. The house took a piece of the ante and chopped five percent of the pot—a nice earn.

My job was as a floor man, watching to make sure there was no cheating and everything ran smoothly. A guy named Nino ran the game. Nino was a native of New York, highly respected and a real professional. We became close friends and remained so for fifteen years until he passed away.

At the end of my first night, Nino asked me to give him a number to play for the next day's numbers drawing. I said 219. He said, "Okay, we're partners for twenty dollars on 219." We played that number every night, but it never hit.

Nino was a lifelong gambler and was always into the shylocks. He played his own numbers with different runners, and one night, he hit for fifteen thousand. The shylocks he owed money to heard about his win and they all showed up to collect. Nino paid them off, and by the next week, he was borrowing again.

Working the poker game was a good job and I made nice money—a G-note ($1,000) a week, plus Nino carrying me as his partner on the 219 numbers bet. If the game got weak (short on players), I'd sit in until another player showed up.

Later on, Mr. Pearl hooked up with another VIP named Vic to open a high-stakes blackjack game. Players could bet as little as five or ten dollars, and there was no limit on the maximum bet.

Vic was an exceptional card player and extremely intelligent. It was said that he was able to memorize every word in the dictionary. At the time, Vic was backing another gambler, a very talented young man named Stu Ungar. Vic took Stu all over to play gin rummy and the kid never lost.

When the blackjack game opened, Mr. Pearl assigned Nino to work there, and I soon joined him as the floor man.

One night I got to work late, and the game had already started. Nino told me there was a sharpie at the table I needed to keep an eye on. I looked the players over and spotted two guys I'd never seen before. One looked to be in his late twenties and I figured him to be the sharpie, Charlie. He was sitting next to a guy who didn't look old enough to be in the game. I didn't know if they were together or just happened to get adjoining seats.

Our rule was that if all the seats weren't full, a player could play two hands. However, he couldn't look at the second hand until he completed his action on the first hand. I saw Charlie very deftly look at the second hand and make a card switch, improving both hands.

I walked over to the table and whispered in his ear, "Sit out the next hand, and come over and talk to me."

He didn't acknowledge me so I went back to my chair and waited. A couple of hands went by and he didn't get up. Back over I went. I whispered, "I said I want to talk to you." This time he looked up at me and nodded.

After that hand, he came over to me. I said, "I saw what you did a few hands ago. If you're going to play two hands, you can't look at the second hand until you're finished with the first. Don't do it again."

He looked at me defiantly and said, "Do you know who I am?"

That pissed me off. I snapped at him, "Do you know who the fuck *I* am, you little prick? If I catch you making a switch again, I'll throw you out the fucking window. Do you understand what I'm telling you?"

Charlie went back to his chair and said something to the young guy next to him. The kid got up and went into the office where Nino was. When he came out, Charlie got up and went in. I saw what was going on, but I kept my cool and stayed in my chair. Nino told me later that the young guy came in the office to assure him he wasn't part of Charlie's play. Charlie then came in to complain about my allegations and the way I talked to him.

Nino said he told Charlie, "If I were you, I wouldn't switch any more cards or make any moves that even look like you're switching. And if Joey said he'd throw you out the fucking window, that's exactly what he'll do, so mind your manners."

The game continued and Charlie tapped out, but the kid did real well. When we closed the game, he said he wanted to treat our crew to breakfast, so Nino, the dealers, the two kitchen girls, and I went to breakfast with him.

The kid sat next to me, stuck out his hand and said, "I'm Stu Ungar. I want to make sure you know I had nothing to do with Charlie's deal."

It turned out the guy I'd thought was too young to even be in the game was already recognized as one of the best card players in the world.

* * *

The night I met Stuey at the game was in 1971 or '72, when he was only eighteen or nineteen. From then on, I spent a lot of time with Stuey both during and after the card games. I also did some research on him and found out exactly how brilliant he was. I remember reading one quote about Stuey that said, "Stuey Ungar is the Bobby Fischer of poker." To be compared to one of the greatest chess players who ever lived is certainly high praise, and in Stuey's case, it was well deserved.

I had been around card players most of my life and there were many good ones in the games I worked. To watch a teenager play against these experienced older guys and beat them regularly was thrilling for me. I can say, without exaggeration, that in my opinion, Stuey was an absolute genius and the ultimate card player.

When Stuey was at the table, he was clearly the master and took over the game through his overwhelming skill. I think one of his most powerful assets was his photographic memory. Playing against Stuey was almost like being in a game against a computer. For example, there is a widely reported incident of when Las Vegas casino owner and gambler Bob Stupak bet Stuey $100,000 that he couldn't name the last cards that would be left in a six-deck shoe used to deal blackjack. Stuey watched as the cards were dealt out, and correctly identified the final cards. Like I said, he was kind of like a computer.

In addition to his knowledge and skill, he was a very aggressive player. When he played Texas Hold 'Em, some described his style of play as bullying, because when he had a big stack of chips, he went after the players with the small stacks and got them out of the game. That was simply smart strategy though.

But I only saw the so-called bullying and aggressiveness exhibited during the games. Away from the table, Stuey was as sweet as apple pie and I really cared for him.

As a youngster, Stuey wasn't an especially good-looking kid. When I first met him, I figured he was probably a virgin. Whether he was or not I'll never know, but one night we took him out and got him initiated just to make sure.

Stuey Ungar seemed to have a lot going for him. He eventually left New York to ply his trade in Las Vegas and was highly successful there. But Sin City and his lifestyle eventually led to his downfall.

* * *

I wasn't with Stuey in Vegas and what I'm going to say next is based primarily on books and articles written about him. However, the stories are written by credible sources such as World Poker Tour co-host and professional poker player Mike Sexton, and the *New York Times*. I believe they accurately portray what happened to Stuey after he left the Big Apple and the tragedy of his death on November 22, 1998, at the age of forty-five.

Stuey won the World Series of Poker Main Event Championship three times—back-to-back in 1980 and 1981, and again in 1997, the year before he died. In those days, the payouts were substantially less than the mega amounts paid today. Even so, his WSOP winnings are listed at $2,081,478 and his overall gambling winnings are estimated to have been as much as $30 million. However, when his body was discovered in a Vegas motel room, only $800 was found, and that was apparently his net worth.

It is widely reported that Stuey's downfall was, in large part, due to drug use—an addiction he supposedly picked up in order to keep up with the demands of his gambling life, which could mean going with little or no sleep for days at a time. I have no reason to doubt the veracity of those stories, but I can say that when I knew Stuey in New York, he wouldn't so much as smoke a cigarette.

According to an article by Mike Sexton, Stuey played in his last poker game on November 11 at the Bellagio. Stuey was "down and out," and a man named Billy Baxter asked Sexton to bring Stuey to his house so he could give him a $25,000 stake to get into the game. Stuey was excited and "was like a happy little kid at the toy store."

At the game, Stuey ended up in a $5,000 freeze-out against a player named Melissa Hayden, and she beat him quite easily. Observers thought Stuey was off his game and played aggressively but impatiently. He cashed out after losing nearly all his money.

To me, it seemed like a sad way to end such a magnificent career.

Stuey's death was officially ruled a heart attack. The coroner commented on the autopsy findings: "The cause is accidental death by coronary atherosclerosis. The heart condition developed over a period of time. The death was brought on by his lifestyle."

Rest in peace, Stuey the Kid.

10 : THE DEALERSHIP

Working for Mr. Pearl was great, but I felt I needed to get a real job. I went to see Tony, an old friend who was a car salesman working at the Bay Cadillac dealership in Astoria, Queens.

He said, "Listen, my good friend Jimmy has an American Motors dealership in Maspeth, Queens. I can call him up and see if he's got an opening."

Jimmy told Tony to have me see him at his dealership the next morning.

When I met Jimmy, I was honest with him. I said, "I've got no experience selling cars. The only thing I've ever sold are health club memberships."

"Don't worry about that right now. What I need is somebody that's aggressive."

"Well, I'm aggressive, but I don't want to bullshit you or embarrass myself."

"I told you not to worry about it. I'm sure you'll do fine."

I went to work for him. The job only lasted about two months, but our friendship has lasted over forty years.

Anyway, I did real well right from the start. The first car I sold was to a guy named Sammy. He and his wife were both deaf mutes. I almost blew the sale because Sammy wanted to start the car he was interested in, but it had been on the showroom floor for so long the battery was dead. *Oh shit!*

One of the other salesmen came to my rescue. He brought in a battery charger and got the car running. Sammy was happy and we made the deal. I didn't know how to fill out the contract so another of my new colleagues helped me with it.

When Jimmy came in the next morning and saw my name in the sales book, he was tickled pink for me.

That day, they cleaned out a room for me to use as my office and I started selling lots of cars—fifteen sold and delivered in the first few weeks. I was actually enjoying myself and making money. I thought maybe I'd found a job that was a good fit for me. Unfortunately, it came to a quick end.

At that dealership, we worked on an "up system." That meant the salesmen took turns greeting potential customers as they walked in the door.

One day when I was up, a guy came in and asked me for directions to the service department. I told him and he went on his way.

Then one of the other salesmen, a little guy who was sort of the shop steward, walked over to me. He said, "You're down."

"Why am I down?"

His voice got louder. "You just spoke to somebody. You're down."

"I gave the guy directions to go to the service area."

Almost hollering, he said, "For the last time, I said you're down."

He turned and walked away and I followed him into his office.

I said, "Don't *ever* talk to me like that again. *Not ever!*"

He started to get loud again. I slapped him across the face so fucking hard that his hairpiece looked like it made a left turn.

I knew I was in big trouble so I went to my office and started taking my personal stuff out of my desk.

The manager came in and said, "Joe, what did you do? You can't do something like that. Please go over and apologize."

"I won't apologize to a piece of shit like him. Forget about it."

As I was walking out, Jimmy came out of his office. "Joe, I'm sorry. What the hell happened?"

I told him and added, "I slapped that little bastard across his face. I don't allow anybody to talk to me like that."

Jimmy was smart enough to know I wasn't the kind of guy to apologize, so he didn't even bother to ask.

I brought my demo (provided car) back the next day. While I was waiting for my ride, I chatted with Jimmy for a few minutes. He said, "Joe, if you ever need to use an office or phone, feel free to stop in. You'll always be welcome here."

Like I said, Jimmy is a friend and a great guy.

* * *

On occasion, I took Jimmy up on his offer, and stopped at the dealership to make a phone call.

One day Jimmy said to me, "Joe, could I see you?" We went into his office and he asked, "Do you know a bookie named Richie?"

I knew of him. He was a decent enough guy, but he was a nobody. I said, "Yeah, I know him. Why?"

"He's been a customer of mine for years. He brought in a friend of his named Marvin, who was looking to buy a car. He said, 'Sell him a car today and he'll bring you the cash in two weeks. I'll stand behind it.' That was over two months ago and I still haven't been paid.

"Marvin owes me eight thousand dollars. Can you help me get it?"

Jimmy gave me Richie's address and the next day I went to his house. He wasn't there, so I left a message with his wife. I told her my name and said I was from the dealership. I asked her to tell her husband I needed to see him and I'd be at the dealership until nine that night.

Around 8:30, I was sitting in my old office when Richie and Marvin showed up. This Marvin was built like a refrigerator—he blocked the whole doorway. I'd seen Arnold Schwarzenegger once and he was a big man. Marvin was bigger.

Richie said, "Hi, Joe. What are you doing here?"

"I'm here because this is my joint."

"Oh, I didn't know that."

"You know it now. Is this Marvin?"

The fridge answered, "Yeah, I'm Marvin."

"You owe me eight thousand dollars. You came in here and bought a car and were supposed to bring the money in two weeks. You didn't bring the fucking money and now it's been two months."

Richie jumped out of his chair and said to Marvin, "Have you got the money for this man? Get him the money!"

As big as he was, Marvin looked scared. He said, "Can I bring a check?"

I didn't even look at Marvin. I said to Richie, "Will his check be good?"

Marvin answered, "It's going to be a check from my wife. It'll be good, I promise."

I said, "Okay, bring it here tomorrow and give it to Jimmy. Make sure you give it to him and nobody else. Okay?"

I stopped in a few days later to make sure Marvin had delivered the check. He had, and Jimmy was ecstatic. He thanked me and said if I ever needed anything all, I had to do was ask.

I said, "Well, I could use a car. The engine in mine blew up, so right now I'm borrowing wheels and bumming rides to get around."

Starting that day, and for the next twenty years, Jimmy provided me with a new car every nine months, including my gas and insurance.

11 : MR. FIXIT

Over the years I'd made a lot of connections from my time at the Copa and my gaming ventures. Some of them did favors for me, and other friends and acquaintances sometimes asked me for help when they were having problems. I found I was able to intervene in certain situations and bring about a resolution before things got out of hand.

THE ABUSER

One time when I was between jobs, a good friend of mine called on me for a favor. He had a sister who was seeing a guy who wasn't very nice. The boyfriend's name was Steve. He was an abuser and had given the girl a real bad beating. My friend wasn't a tough guy, so he came to me and told me the story. He wanted me to teach the guy a lesson.

I checked around to make sure Steve wasn't somebody important or wasn't connected to anybody important. My information was that he wasn't. I also found out he hung around a joint off Sutphin Boulevard in Jamaica, Queens.

I asked Billy, another friend, to go with me when I went to see Steve. When we walked into the place, there were three derelict-looking guys at the bar, and another at a table reading a newspaper. I figured the guy at the table was the most likely to be Steve.

While Billy stayed by the door to keep an eye on the guys at the bar and any new arrivals, I walked over to the table.

I asked, "Are you Steve?"

"Yes," he said, and stood up.

As soon as he got to his feet, I hit him, and kept hitting him until he went down to the floor, blood coming from his nose, mouth, and cuts around both eyes. He was a mess.

Nobody had come in and the three guys at the bar never moved. Billy and I walked out with Steve still sprawled on the floor, blood pooling under his face.

At that time, I lived in a big house in Flushing on a dead-end street that was very private and quiet. The only other house on the block was the man across from me. Any car coming in there had to be for either me or my neighbor.

The day after I gave Steve the beating, my wife asked me to drive to an Italian deli on Parsons Boulevard to get her some cold cuts. When I got back, there was an unmarked police car parked on the street. I figured Steve must have filed a complaint against me. I backed out and waited.

A few minutes later, a couple of detectives came out of my door, got into their car, and drove away. When I went inside, my wife was nervous. She told me the cops had been there looking for me. I assured her I bumped into them on the street and everything was fine. There was nothing to worry about. After calming her down, I drove to Corona to meet Billy.

He said, "Don was here looking for you. Vince wants to see you."

Vince was a VIP in the neighborhood. He was a great guy and he seemed to really like me. Don was his driver.

I figured I'd better see what Vince wanted first, and worry about Steve and the cops later.

When I got to Vince's, he invited me to sit down and have a cup of espresso with him.

We were making small talk when he hit me with, "Do you know a guy named Steve?"

When a man like Vince asks you a question, it's smart to answer quickly and honestly. "Yes."

"Do you know who he is?"

"No."

I knew then my research on Steve had missed something.

Vince explained, "He's someone's nephew, and that someone is a friend of mine."

He then told me Steve's version of what happened. It was pretty accurate, except Steve hadn't told him about the beating he gave his girlfriend—which was the catalyst for the whole thing.

Vince then gave me a chance to tell my side. I told him everything, including why Steve got the beating.

Vince nodded. "But if you knew who his uncle was, you shouldn't have done it."

"I apologize for not knowing about Steve's uncle, that was my error."

And then I decided to take a shot. I said, "I don't understand something. If Steve went to his uncle about this, why did two cops come to my house this morning to pick me up? Does his uncle know about that?"

Vince just looked at me. I thought I saw a slight smile on his face; at least I hoped it was a smile.

Vince told Don to call his friend in Jamaica and tell him we were on our way over for a sit down.

Half an hour later, we were all sitting in a club in Jamaica—me, Don, Vince, Steve, and his uncle. Steve looked like crap, but I didn't care. Anybody who hits a woman *should* look bad.

The uncle already had Steve's story, and I gave him my side, including the beating of his girlfriend and the cops coming for me. The part about Steve going to the cops really upset his uncle. Guys like him handle their own problems; they don't run to the law.

Steve may have been an asshole, but he wasn't stupid. He blamed his wife for calling the cops.

I assured the uncle that the incident had been a mistake and not a sign of disrespect to him. He was satisfied. The complaint made to the cops would be dropped and the matter was closed.

Vince gave me a stern warning on the way back to Corona. "You'd better be careful, and you'd better keep your nose clean."

* * *

DISCO FEVER

I was friends with a VIP named John, who ran an illegal gambling operation. I had a little problem and had to leave town for a while. When I came back, I had trouble finding a job. John helped me get a gig and eventually hired me to work his blackjack game.

John had a girlfriend named Molly, who owned a disco in the very affluent Westchester County, and in the late 1970s, discos were the rage. Molly was having trouble with teenagers and other young people coming into her joint and causing problems. She asked John to help her out and he referred me to straighten things out for her.

The place was huge. Four guys worked the door and four more worked inside, plus the bartenders. There were two bars—one just inside the door with two bartenders, and a second, larger bar in the back with four or five bartenders working on the weekends, and five girls waitressing.

When I met with Molly, she asked, "What is your pay?"

"I have a partner and we get a hundred and fifty each, per night."

"Ouch! That's too expensive for me."

"That's okay. It's been nice meeting you and good luck." I started to walk away.

"Wait a minute. Where are you going?"

"I told you what the pay is. You said you couldn't afford it and we won't work for any less. There doesn't seem to be anything else to talk about."

"I've changed my mind. John said you're very good and I'll pay what you asked."

Then she told me about the guy who caused her the most problems. Billy Upazz. He was of legal age and a real bad kid.

On my first night, I told the guys working the door to stop Billy if he tried to come in and tell him I wanted to talk with him. With guys like Billy, it's important to read them the rules before they get inside. Once they are in, it can take a lot of effort to remove them.

About two hours later, one of the doormen came to me and said Billy was there. They hadn't stopped him at the door though; he was already inside and at the back bar. That meant I'd have to get him from the bar, through the whole place, and out the front door. He'd probably have friends in the place, making it embarrassing to him, and if he resisted, they might join in. I wasn't happy, but it was what it was.

I went into the bar and asked one of the bartenders to point Billy out to me. He was another one of those guys built like an icebox.

I walked over to him and said, "I'd like to talk to you in private."

He said defiantly, "If you want to talk, we can do it right here."

"It's too loud. We'll have trouble hearing each other. Let's go out front."

"You don't think you're going to walk me out of here, do you?"

"No. I just want to talk in private."

I started walking toward the front and he followed me until we got outside.

I said, "If you want to go back inside, you can. But you've got to understand: you can't get drunk, can't abuse people, or start fights. You have to respect my place and me. As long as you follow the rules, we won't have any problem."

"I understand."

We shook hands and he went back inside. Not only did I never have any issues with Billy, later that night when I had an altercation with some other people, he was right there to help me out.

Billy later became a professional boxer, but he wouldn't train and didn't last very long.

Anyway, I had my partner Frank Zappella with me, whom I'd trust with my life, and now Billy, who was a monster. So I was feeling pretty secure working the disco, but that wasn't where my next problem came from.

ROAD RAGE

A couple of weeks later, I was driving down Northern Boulevard in Woodside on my way to work when a car cut me off. I slammed on my brakes and avoided hitting him. I caught up with him at the next light, pulled alongside, and rolled my window down.

"What's wrong with you, cutting in front of me like that?" I hollered.

He was an Oriental guy. He gave me the finger and said, "Go fuck yourself."

When the light changed, I pulled in front of him and stopped. I went to his car, and he got out and started throwing wild punches at me. I hit him a couple of times, then caught him with a left hook and he went down, but in the process, I broke my thumb. I didn't realize then it was broken, only that it hurt like hell.

Frank Zappella lived nearby and I went to his house. He examined my thumb and must have thought I'd dislocated it, because he grabbed onto it and yanked. It hurt so bad I almost pissed my pants.

Then he said, "I think it's broke."

I went to the hospital emergency room and after a long wait, got to see a doctor. He confirmed the break and started working on me. After a few minutes, he made a phone call, then came back and did a little more. He stopped again and went back to the phone. That's when it dawned on me. He was calling another doctor and getting instructions on what to do. *Holy shit!*

When he finally finished, he said, "I suggest you see your own doctor because that thumb may have to be reset."

That took place on a Saturday. When I saw my doctor on Monday, the thumb had to be pinned and reset and put in a cast. I feel sorry for any other poor soul who was treated by that ER doctor.

That night there was a knock on my door and a cop was there with an arrest warrant for me for assaulting the other driver. I didn't want to upset my wife, so I went upstairs and told her I had to go with a friend of mine to take care of some business and I'd be back soon.

I told the cop I didn't want to start a buzz in the neighborhood, so I'd appreciate it if he took me out to his car without cuffing me. I gave him a hundred dollars and he left the cuffs off.

Before we left, he told me what the other driver said and asked for my version. I admitted hitting the guy, but said he started throwing punches first.

The cop said, "Good. When we get to the station, tell the sergeant the other guy hit you first."

"He swung at me but nothing landed."

"I know that, but tell the sergeant what I told you. That way you can swear out a complaint against him too."

I changed my story slightly, as the cop suggested. When we went to court, the judge asked the other guy what happened and he gave his version. Next it was my turn.

After I finished, the judge said to me, "So he hit you first?"

"That's right, Your Honor."

"How old are you, Mr. Silvestri?"

"I'm fifty-three, Your Honor."

He turned to the Oriental. "And how old are you?"

"I'm twenty."

"You're a twenty-year-old man and you fought with a fifty-three-year-old. You should be ashamed of yourself."

The judge's rant was all the more funny because the kid had a knot on his head and a black eye, yet the judge was treating him like the bully.

The judge threw the case out and I left his courtroom a happy man.

* * *

A REAL SCRAPPER

I got involved with a scrapyard located near Shea Stadium. I'd known Mike, the owner, for years and he'd borrowed some money from a guy who was really taking advantage of him, charging him three points a week interest on the loan.

If you're not familiar with points, here's how it works. Let's say you borrow a thousand dollars at three points. That means you pay three hundred dollars a week just in interest—nothing on the principal. That goes on, week after week, until you're able to pay off the thousand dollars. Multiply that for each additional thousand dollars you borrow and that's your weekly interest payment. It's outrageous.

I said, "When does this guy come to collect?"

"He's always here on Thursday."

"I'll be there next week and talk with him."

The following Thursday, I was at the scrapyard when the lender came in. He knew me from the neighborhood and said, "Joey, what are you doing here?"

"I'm here now, I'm partners with Mike."

"I didn't know you and Mike are partners."

"We've been keeping it kind of quiet, but you know now. I'm glad you stopped in because I want to talk to you about the money situation."

Right away, he got defensive. "I can't talk with you about that, Joey, because it's not my money. I'm just the middleman."

"That's okay. Whoever's money it is, I want to talk with them."

"Let me see what I can do and I'll get back to you."

"You do that."

He didn't, but I knew who the guy behind him was, and we were friends. I went directly to him and told him the story.

He said, "From now on deal with me and not that other guy."

The interest was dropped from three points to one, which is what it should have been from the beginning. The principal got paid off in a fairly short time.

Mike was so appreciative that we actually did become partners.

One day when I came in, Mike was talking on the phone with a guy named Ernie, who lived in New Jersey. Mike and Ernie were very close and Mike asked me to get on the line and hear what Ernie had to say.

Ernie seemed very nervous as he told me his story. He ran a junkyard and had a new machine—the only one in New Jersey at the time—that was about three stories high and could separate all the materials from the cars being scrapped. It sorted copper, aluminum, tin, and other metals, saving a lot of manual labor.

He said three guys had come to see him. They took him outside away from his family and told him they would throw first his daughter, then his son, and then his wife into the machine while he watched unless he did exactly what they wanted. They said they'd be back in a few days to give him his orders. I told Ernie that when they came back, he should have them call me.

It turned out the guys threatening Ernie were with one of the five families and I knew their boss. When he called me, I asked to have a sit down with him.

We met and he explained how he and his crew got involved with Ernie. The background was Ernie had a partner who was also in the cemetery monument business. He wanted to push Ernie out of the junkyard and have both businesses for himself. He figured if these guys could take control of the junkyard from Ernie, they'd turn it over to him and he'd just have to give them a little piece of the business.

What a fucking idiot this guy was. If those guys took over the place, there was no way it would ever end up in the partner's hands. They'd have pushed Ernie out and him too.

After a long conversation, the guy told me he was sorry his crew got involved and promised Ernie and his family would be left alone. We shook hands on it and then he asked, "Do you think there is any way we can get rid of this monument guy?"

I said, "I don't give a fuck about him. You can put him in one of his own fucking monuments as far as I'm concerned."

In the end, they got a piece of the monument business.

* * *

HAND GRENADE

One day, my old friend Jimmy from the American Motors dealership called me and said he needed to see me right away. When I got there, he said, "I've got a problem, Joey. There's a girl working in the parts department who has a very jealous boyfriend. He thinks she's having an affair with one of the salesmen and he's threatening to blow up the showroom with a hand grenade."

I didn't take it too serious because most guys who really intend to do something don't announce it ahead of time, but I told Jimmy to get the girl on the phone for me. We talked for a minute and then she said her boyfriend's name was Mitchell and gave me his phone number.

I got him on the line, introduced myself, and said, "Mitchell, I understand you're coming here with a hand grenade to blow up my showroom, is that right?"

"I'm going to do a lot worse. I'm going to blow up the whole place and everybody in it. Do you hear me?"

I said, "I heard you. Now I want you to listen to me very carefully, you piece of shit. I want you to come here right now. Make sure you bring the hand grenade because I'm going to shove it right up your ass."

The line went silent.

I called the girl back and told her, "I don't think Mitchell will bother you again. If he does, tell Jimmy and I'll take care of it from there."

Mitchell didn't cause any further problems.

* * *

These and other similar incidents gave me confidence I was able to handle most any situation. It was a good thing too, because I was about to get into a situation that proved tough to get out of.

12 : MICHAEL HELLERMAN

I was working at the health club when a big, mean-looking guy I'd never seen before showed up in the doorway. He asked if I was Joe "Savestri." Even though he was off a little on my last name, I nodded. He didn't say anything more, just turned and walked away. It turned out he was an advance scout for my next visitor.

This time, the guy at my door was somebody I remembered very well. He went by the nickname of Little Davey. I hadn't seen Davey in years because he'd been sent away for a twenty spot and had just been released from prison. Although he wasn't a very big man, he was a giant in the eyes of his peers in the rackets and had a near-genius IQ.

After some small talk, he said, "Joe, the apartment I'm going to move into won't be ready for a couple of weeks. I know you're affiliated with the hotel here, and wonder if there is any chance you can get the hotel people to let me stay until my place is ready?"

I took him to the Shelton Hotel desk and made the arrangements. While Little Davey stayed at the hotel, we spent a lot of time together and our relationship continued after he moved into his own place. He really liked me because he knew I could take care of myself and thought I had a good head for business. As time passed, we became even closer and did a few things together that made us some pretty good money.

And then I found out the health club's lease wasn't going to be renewed and I would eventually be out of a full-time job. Little Davey told Jack Pearl about my situation and said if Jack could use me elsewhere, he'd appreciate it. Mr. Pearl's card games weren't going that well. The blackjack game was pretty much shut down and the poker games were really slow. However, he was a man of many resources and liked me and my work.

When I went to the poker game the following Friday night, Mr. Pearl called me into his office. He said he was sorry to hear about the health club and then asked me what I thought about Murray, the guy who ran the numbers out of the card games and also did some shylocking. As far as I knew, he was doing a good business. Murray was in his seventies then, but looked a lot older. I thought he was a decent guy and told Mr. Pearl that.

"Joey, have you heard that Murray's driver just passed away?"

Murray never drove anywhere himself, he always had a driver. "Yes, I guess I did hear something about it," I said. "Why?"

"I thought you might be interested in being his new driver. Are you?"

I wanted to be known as a guy who would do any job necessary, and this sounded like a good opportunity for me. "Yes, I'm interested."

"Good. Meet Murray at 45th Street and Seventh Avenue at ten o'clock Monday morning."

I showed up as scheduled, parked my car, and met Murray on the street. We went into a restaurant and talked over a cup of coffee. Murray explained that I'd work six days a week and make a hundred dollars a day. We'd eat lunch out on occasion and sometimes dinner as well.

Murray had to have his numbers collected and turned in to the Irish guys on the Westside by 3:30 p.m., after which he'd hang out in the poker room for a while. If the game was light on players, he'd sit in until the seats filled up, but he was mainly there to lend money to the gamblers who ran short on cash.

I thought things were going pretty well until one evening at the card game, Mr. Pearl called me into his office.

He asked, "How are things with you and Murray?"

The question made me uncomfortable. "Good, as far as I know."

"Murray sees it different, Joey. He says that by the time he pays his expenses, including your two hundred a day, there isn't a lot left."

I didn't call Murray a liar, but I looked Mr. Pearl in the eye and said, "I get *a hundred* a day and Murray is supposed to cover my parking fees, which he never does."

"I see. That's all, Joey. Tell Nino I need to talk with him."

After a few minutes, Nino came out and it was my turn again in Mr. Pearl's office.

"Joey, if you want to take over Murray's numbers business, I can't stop you. If he complains to me, I'll just tell him you're not with me on that. You're with Davey and there's nothing I can do. After that, there's nowhere else Murray can go. That's it—cut and dried."

I knew what I had to do. On my way home, I went to Brooklyn and talked with Jimmy "Nap" Napoli. He was with the Genovese family and was one of the most respected VIPs in New York, a real classy guy. He ran a huge illegal gambling empire that stretched all the way to Las Vegas. When I first got involved with the numbers at the age of nineteen, he was the guy I turned my work in to.

Jimmy remembered me and I explained my situation to him. I told him I was going to inherit a lucrative numbers business that was currently being run out of the Westside and I was looking to switch. I asked if he was interested in doing business with me.

Jimmy said, "I've got one question. This business you're taking over, does it come with problems?"

"No, no problems at all."

"Okay. I haven't been taking anybody on, but I'll take you, Joey."

The next morning, I met Murray as usual. We made our last pickup of the day at three o'clock from a runner named Izzy. When Izzy handed the envelope to Murray, I grabbed it from him.

I said, "Izzy, from now on you'll be dealing with me. This is no longer Murray's business—it's mine."

Murray's expression was one of total shock, while Izzy's was confusion. He kept looking at Murray for guidance. I said, "Izzy, do you understand what I just told you? From now on, you're working for me."

Izzy got the message. "Sure, Joe, I understand."

I was back in the numbers racket.

* * *

One day I was at a place on Mulberry Street to meet Davey when he called on the phone. He wanted me to meet him back at the health club in an hour. When I got there, we had a cup of coffee and then Davey said, "Let's take a walk." He had a thing about discussing business inside buildings and preferred to talk outside whenever possible.

On the street, he said, "I got a message from one of my friends in prison—Johnny Dio. I've known him since childhood and he wants me to do him a favor."

"Is it something I can help you with?"

"Yes. He has someone he needs to have looked after. He wants to make sure nobody bothers this person or causes him any problems. That will mean spending a lot of time with the guy. Is that something you can do for me?"

I knew that when a VIP wanted someone "looked after," it was usually because he had information that could hurt the VIP. It wasn't something I was really excited about, but you didn't turn down a request from a guy like Little Davey.

"Sure," I said, "I'm glad to help."

The next day, Davey introduced me to Michael Hellerman. He was a master con man and stock swindler. He even wrote a book about his exploits titled *Wall Street Swindler*. Davey told Michael I'd be with him every day and take him wherever he needed to go. If he had any problems, he should bring them to my attention.

From then on, I'd call Michael every morning and arrange for a time to pick him up and take him around to appointments and business meetings. Sometimes he wouldn't let me come inside the restaurants with him and had me wait in the car. I figured he was probably talking private business so that was okay with me. However, we found out later that Michael was a government informant and he may very well have been meeting with his handlers while I waited outside.

Anyway, Michael was a big man—around six feet tall and 250 pounds or better—but he wasn't in good shape. He was a personable guy though, very smart and smooth, and overall, we got along pretty well. The things about him that I didn't care for were he loved to have an audience and he spoke very loudly.

One day, Michael told me he wanted to go to the Copa because Don Rickles was opening there and he was a big Rickles fan. Little Davey told Michael I had connections at the Copa and he wanted to know if I'd take him. I called the Copa and made arrangements for Michael, his girlfriend (Michael also had a wife), and me to see Rickles' show that night.

We had a table near ringside and were waiting for the show to start when mobster Joey "Crazy Joey" Gallo and his party took the table right behind us. At that time, Joey was in hot water with other New York mobsters and the word on the street was he was a good guy to keep away from.

Joey noticed me, waved, and told the waiter to bring a bottle of wine for our table. I very nicely told him we weren't drinking and turned down his offer.

After the show, we went upstairs to the restaurant for some Chinese food; Michael loved Chinese and the Copa still had the best Chinese food in New York. We had just placed our order when Joey Gallo walked over to our table. The first words out of his mouth were about Michael's girlfriend. "Is she a wife or a *goomah* (mistress)?"

I didn't want to be around Gallo to begin with, and his question didn't sit well with me. I kept my cool though, and let it slide.

Gallo then said, "We're going to Umberto's to celebrate my birthday and have some good Italian food. Why don't you come along?"

Michael got all excited and was ready to accept the offer. He started to get up from the table, but I grabbed his leg and held it down as I said to Gallo, "We appreciate the invitation, but we just ordered here, so we'll have to pass."

Gallo shrugged. "Okay. If you change your mind, you're welcome to join us later," he said and then left.

We had our meal and hung around the Copa until near closing time. We found out the next day that Joey Gallo had been gunned down at Umberto's in an apparent Mob hit. It was April 7, 1972, and he had just turned forty-three. Had we accepted his invitation, we might very well have been dead too.

* * *

One night a few months later, Michael and I were out pretty late. I dropped him off and drove home, figuring my day was over—it wasn't though. I was barely inside my door when my phone rang. I very seldom received calls at that time of night and feared it had to be bad news.

It was.

"Joey, you've gotta get over here right away!" Michael screamed. "Did you hear me? I said right away!"

"Calm down and tell me what's wrong," I said.

"My house has been shot up. They machine-gunned my fuckin' house!"

I ended the call quickly because I didn't want anything said that might be of interest to unwanted listeners. "Okay, I'll be right over."

I drove to Bayside and parked about a block from Michael's place. Police cars with lights flashing were parked up and down the block, and cops on foot were all over the place. There was nothing I'd be able to do there to help Michael, and it made no sense for me to involve myself at the crime scene so I headed back home.

According to news reports, Michael told the police he was the victim of an attack by mobsters. However, a second version of the incident began to circulate on the streets almost immediately that Michael had arranged the shooting himself for unknown reasons. To this day, I don't know for sure which is true, but I tend to believe it was an inside job.

Anyway, the next day I talked with Davey and he told me to continue to do what I'd been doing. Michael wanted to leave New York though, claiming the Mob was after him and things were getting too hot for him to stick around. Before he could move, the law got in the way. During the last conversation I had with Michael, he told me about it.

"Joey, I worked out a deal with the prosecutor over those charges that have been hanging over my head. I'm going to have to do some time and I don't know if I can handle it."

"How much time?"

"Three months."

"What do you mean you don't know if you can do it? You can do three months standing on your head."

"You don't understand, Joey. I'll have cellmates, and I can't go to the bathroom if somebody is watching me. I don't know what I'm going to do."

I managed not to laugh. I thought for a few seconds, then told him something to make him feel better. "I'll tell you what. I'll take care of that problem for you."

"How, Joey? How can you do it?"

"You know I've got connections, right?"

"Yeah, I know you do."

"Okay, so when you know you're going to have to use the toilet, tell the guards you have to make a phone call. Call me and I'll make sure your cellmates are removed while you do your business."

The relief was obvious in his voice when he said, "Joey, that was the only thing I was worried about. Now I'll be able to do it standing on my head like you said."

When I told Davey about it, we both had a good laugh and I thought I'd heard the last of Michael Hellerman. I was wrong though.

A few days later, a car pulled up while I was on the street waiting for Davey. Some suits got out, and one of them said, "Are you Joe Silvestri?"

"Yes, I am."

He flashed his badge and ordered me into their car.

"Am I under arrest?" I asked.

"Just get into the car like you were told."

They drove me to an office building in Midtown and took me to a small office on the sixth floor. After a couple minutes, a very stern-looking, tall man with gray hair came in and sat down behind the desk. He asked, "Are you Joe Silvestri?"

"Yes. Am I under arrest?"

He glared at me. "Let's get something straight. I'll ask the questions and you'll answer them. Understand?"

I nodded.

He looked at some papers and photos on the desk and asked, "Do you know Michael Hellerman?"

"Yes."

"Are you his bodyguard?"

"No."

"Do you carry a gun?"

"No."

"Are you a member of organized crime?"

"No."

"What is your relationship with Michael Hellerman?"

"He's a friend."

"Did you hear what happened to Michael Hellerman's house?"

"I read about it in the newspaper."

"Do you think the Mob is trying to kill Michael Hellerman?"

"I don't know."

"What is your opinion?"

"I really don't have one."

"When was the last time you saw Michael Hellerman?"

"I think it was two days ago."

"Do you think Michael Hellerman is still alive?"

"I certainly hope so."

At that point, the guy got up and walked out of the room and the suit followed him. The suit came back in a couple minutes and said, "Okay, you can go. Do you want us to drive you?"

I said, "No thanks" and walked out the door.

During the subway ride back downtown, I reflected on the interview and was satisfied I handled it properly. In my mind, I was now free of Michael.

I wasn't though. He had a connection to one more incident that could have resulted in my death.

13 : THE CHECK

Shortly after the cops turned me loose, I got word that Davey wanted me to meet him at the health club. We walked down Lexington and turned east onto 47th Street, on which traffic was one-way westbound. Davey liked that because the cars were always coming toward us and it was easy to spot suspicious vehicles. Davey took an additional precaution by always having a cigarette in his mouth when he talked, so lip readers would have a difficult time knowing what he was saying.

I told Davey all about my session with the cops—what they asked, what I answered. He didn't say anything right away, and when he did speak, he said, "I'm pretty sure the shit is going to hit the fan. I'm going to keep a low profile and you should do the same. I think it will be best if you get out of town for a while and don't come back until I tell you it's okay."

Davey didn't provide any more details and I didn't ask. I knew he'd told me all he felt I needed to know. We agreed that messages between us would be handled through a liquor store whose owner was a friend of ours.

After we split up, I called my lifelong friend Billy Katz. I told him something was up and I had to leave town. Billy said he knew a small motel in Miami off the beaten track and it would be perfect for me to lay low. Billy offered to come with me and we caught a flight to Florida.

Billy was right. The motel was comfortable, but didn't have a lot of frills and didn't attract attention. It was ideal for my purposes.

We were in Miami for a couple of weeks when I called the liquor store to see what was going on. To my surprise, Davey was there and got on the line. He said things were clear and for me to return to New York. When I got in, we'd meet at Jack Pearl's restaurant in the Bronx. Billy and I hopped on a plane. We were back in the city late that afternoon and at the restaurant around six o'clock. Davey wasn't there, nor was Mr. Pearl. I asked Sonny, the restaurant host, where I could find a secure phone. He directed me to a payphone at a gas station down the street. I went there and called Davey. He told me to go back to the restaurant, have something to eat, and he'd be there in an hour or so.

About halfway through the meal, Mr. Pearl came in and joined Billy and me. We made some small talk and he told us some entertaining stories. When we finished eating, he insisted we have some of his cheesecake. I'm a dessert guy and cheesecake is one of my favorites. I said to him, "I'm a gourmet when it comes to cheesecake and it takes a lot to impress me."

Mr. Pearl looked me straight in the eye and said, "If this isn't the best cheesecake you've ever eaten, I'll buy you a suit and maybe even throw in a tie."

It came from Eileen's Special Cheesecake and I've got to say, that to this day, it was the best cheesecake I've ever had.

I was having a great day and figured it would continue. However, everything changed when Davey came in.

* * *

Davey didn't arrive alone; he had a guy named Roger with him. It turned out that Roger was associated with another crew. Mr. Pearl excused himself, and normally at this point, Billy would have also left the table. Davey really liked and trusted Billy though, so he was allowed to stay.

Davey got right to the point. "Joey, when was the last time you saw those two guys Richie and Albert?"

At first I drew a blank. "Richie and Albert?"

Davey refreshed my memory. "You know who I'm talking about and they don't like you."

I knew them. They were a couple of low-life characters from the neighborhood who always wanted to be somebodies and would never make it. They were jealous of me and tried to get me into problems by spreading lies about me. Their plans backfired, and they got into a lot of trouble themselves and had to get out of town. I hadn't heard of them since. Apparently they were back.

"Oh yeah. The ones I had a problem with in the Village a year or year and a half ago. That was the last time I saw them."

Davey turned to Roger. "Tell Joey what's going on."

Roger said, "Joey, I've known Davey all my life. I don't have to be here, but I came out of respect for Davey and his feelings toward you. Just understand that I'm only a messenger."

I nodded. "Go ahead."

Roger said, "This Richie and Albert met with my friend Nicky Black's brother-in-law. They told him you got hold of a check in the amount of a $100,000 that was intended for Nicky. They said you kept it, signed it, and cashed it."

Nicky Black was a captain of one of the street crews—a very tough guy. I'd known him for twenty years and we'd always gotten along okay. His brother-in-law was a different story though. He was drunk one night at Mr. Pearl's poker game and became loud and obnoxious. Mr. Pearl told me to get him in line and I did. But even though I was nice about it, he resented me and hated my guts.

I said to Davey, "I never got any check." Next, I told Roger, "Richie and Albert, huh? Anything you hear about me that comes from those two pieces of shit has to be a lie."

He responded, "Joey, the check had your signature on it and you supposedly cashed it."

I said, "It might be that this check you're talking about has what is *supposed* to be my signature on it. What I'm telling you is that I never saw that check or signed it. I sure as hell didn't cash it."

Davey said to Roger, "Okay, that's all for today. I'll get back to you tomorrow."

Then we all shook hands and Roger left.

Davey asked me, "Do you know anything about this check business?"

"Not a thing. This is the first I've heard about it. What I should have asked Roger is where that check is now. Do you know who has it?"

"No, but you'll have a chance to ask that question when we meet with Nicky Black. I'm scheduling a sit down with him and his brother-in-law."

* * *

Two nights later, Davey and I drove to Nicky Black's restaurant on Hudson Street. Nicky and his brother-in-law were seated at a secluded table by themselves and we joined them. Due to the brother-in-law being there, Davey and I didn't order anything—not even coffee. The brother-in-law was the enemy and you don't break bread with the enemy.

Nicky started the conversation by asking Davey, "Do you know what's going on with this check thing?"

Because Roger had given Davey and me a heads up out of respect, we had to feign ignorance. "No," Davey said. "I'm totally in the dark."

I don't know if Nicky believed that, but to question it would have meant calling Davey a liar and that was something nobody did.

Nicky addressed himself to Davey and related the same story about the check we'd heard from Roger. He finished with, "Somehow Joey got the check, signed it, cashed it and took *my* money." He spoke that final sentence as he stared right at me.

Davey asked, "Nicky, how sure are you that Joey did these things you're saying?"

"The information is from a very reliable source."

"But, Nicky, how many times over the years have these so-called reliable sources turned out to be not so reliable? Maybe this source doesn't like Joey or told someone who doesn't like Joey. Then they come to you and spin this tale."

Nicky didn't budge. "I said this source is *very* reliable."

Davey turned to me. "Joey, do you know anything about this check?"

"Absolutely not."

"Do you have any idea why somebody would make up a story like this?"

Again I said, "Absolutely not."

Davey told Nicky, "If you want to ask Joey anything yourself, go ahead."

Nicky turned to me. "You never saw that check, never signed it, and didn't cash it?"

"I never saw the check and didn't sign it."

"But, Joey, it had your signature on it."

I said, as calmly as I could, "Nicky, if my name is on that check, it was forged. Had it somehow gotten into my hands, I'd have taken it to Davey and we'd have brought it to you. Never in a million years would I have kept it. I would never be that disrespectful to you or Davey. If you can produce that check and it has my actual signature on it, you can skin me with a rusty razor blade."

Davey said to me, "Joey, go to the bar and get a drink. I'll be with you in a few minutes."

As I got up from the table, Nicky told his brother-in-law, "Go outside and have a smoke while Davey and I talk."

A few minutes later, Davey and Nicky walked over to the bar. Nicky shook my hand and said, "Thanks for coming." That was it; the sit down was over.

The efforts by Richie, Albert, and the brother-in-law to get me clipped failed and I never heard another word about me being involved with that fucking check.

What is interesting, though, is I later found out the check ended up in the possession of Mike Hellerman and he got it with the permission of the feds. How in the hell that happened, I'll never know. All I do know is that I was finally through with Mike.

14 : THE CHEF, THE BUTCHER, & THE DONALD

THE CHEF

Joe Babbington and I have been friends for over thirty years. We first met when Joe was trying to open a restaurant, but his credit was borderline, and he was having trouble getting a loan. I had a friend who ran a venture capital company and was giving out legitimate money at a very cheap price. My guy had to stretch to the limit, but he was able to give Joe the loan. Joe and I have been friends and business partners ever since.

We opened a couple of small places together. Our arrangement was that Joe—who was an excellent chef, there was nothing relating to food he couldn't do—would be master of the kitchen. I'd run the bar and function as manager.

I think it was around the early to mid-1990s that we ran into an opportunity buy a real nice place in Chelsea on Ninth Avenue between 22nd and 23rd streets. We got a hell of a deal on it because the owner was an Italian guy who had the habit of betting on the horses. Like many gamblers, he ran into financial troubles and needed some money quick. Joe negotiated a price that gave the owner the money he needed, but was also a real bargain for us. We named it Babbington's. With Joe working his magic in the kitchen and me behind the bar, how could we miss?

We transitioned from Italian to American cuisine, the food was great, and the business really took off. Besides the quality of the food, there were several soap opera stars living in the area. When they stopped in, we treated them the way we should, and they started coming in regularly, further boosting business.

The only downside of the area was a lot of people there were dying from AIDS. The disease was reaching its peak and there were a lot of gay people living there. Some of those who died were our customers—nice young men. We held memorials for them when they passed. It was a very sad thing.

The bar was twelve feet long and seated seven; the tables could handle another seventy-five. We were always jammed and often had to have a waiting line. Some people complained about the wait and went elsewhere. We didn't like it either, but that's the way it was.

One night I was in the middle of the bar mixing a drink when this little elderly lady came up and asked me, "Excuse me, are you the manager?"

"Yes, I am. How can I help you?"

"I'm seated over there," she said, nodding toward the booth next to the door to the kitchen. "My waiter is in the kitchen and I need to call him to add something to my order, but I'm not sure of his name. When he seated me he said his name was Bob. But the guy in the kitchen keeps calling him Cocksucker Face."

That was Joe. He didn't mean anything by it, that was just the way he talked. About every other word out of his mouth was some sort of profanity.

* * *

THE PROMO

I was doing the promo for the restaurant and thought I'd invite Bob Lape, the restaurant and food critic from a local TV station, to stop in and do a review of the place. He and his cameraman came in on a weekend. I showed them to a table and left them to place their orders. By pure chance, the people at the table next to them were raving about how good the food was. Bob later complimented me about that and said the food was great. Still, I can't help but think he might have suspected it was a setup.

A few minutes later, I heard Joe yelling like a lunatic in the kitchen. I ran from the bar to the kitchen door to see what was going on. There was Bob, with his cameraman, trying to interview Joe and photograph the kitchen. Joe wasn't going for it and was telling them so as only he could.

I told Bob there would be no interviews or photos in the kitchen that night. They left and we never got a review. The only good thing was that at least he didn't pan us.

* * *

THE IRISHMAN

One night I came in early to take care of the bar and manage things while Joe was with a guy planning a party. This huge Irish-looking guy, tall and very muscular, came in. He ordered a beer and drank it, then another. When he finished that one, he said in a very loud, gruff voice, "What the fuck kind of bar is this? I don't think it's an Irish bar and it's not a Guinea bar. Is it a nigger bar?"

With that, I took his glass and threw it in the trash. I said, "Now get the fuck out of here and don't come back."

He walked to the door and before leaving, turned around and said, "I've been thrown out of better places than this."

After he left, I went down to the end of the bar to talk with two of my regular customers, Teddy Williams and his girlfriend Miranda. Teddy was black and she was Spanish. Teddy was a great guy and I felt bad about the jerk's comment.

"Don't worry about it," Teddy said. "I've dealt with that stuff all my life. That guy is a real asshole. He's been kicked out of about every bar in the neighborhood—even the Irish pubs."

I didn't think any more about it that night, but a couple of nights later, the two guys who owned the Irish joint down the street came in. One of them said, "I heard that big Irish dope was in here. I want you to know I want no part of him and we threw him out of our place."

He continued, "He's a big blowhard and a bad drunk. He has no adult friends, only young punks who hang around with him because they figure he's a tough guy. Every time he goes into a bar, he asks if it's Irish. If it's not, he starts throwing insults. Then he gets his young buddies into fights but he never participates himself."

The following Saturday night, we had a full house and the place was really jumping. On the right side of the room, next to the window, we had a table for six. It was a nice place to sit and gave the customers a great view of what was going on outside. That particular night, a black judge and his family were seated there.

The door opened. The troublemaker stuck his head in and said, "I knew this was a nigger bar."

I jumped over the bar, and as I did, he took off at a run. The two kids he had with him weren't as quick. My waiter got into a tussle with one of them and I knocked the other one on his ass. The Irishman stopped halfway down the block and started screaming, "It's a nigger bar! It's a nigger bar!"

Somebody told Joe what was going on and he came out and got into the melee we were having with the two punks. In the meantime, the Irishman made his getaway. The pub owner was right about him: he avoided getting into the physical stuff himself. We never saw the bastard again after that night.

After things calmed down, I told Joe about the first time the Irishman came in and what the pub owners told me about him. A few days later, we stopped at their place and bought a round for the bar. It was the right thing to do.

* * *

THE BUTCHER

I first met Sam Solasz when I was working at the health club in Forest Hills. He was a very intelligent man, but sometimes had trouble communicating because of his heavy Polish accent. He was always smiling and had a great personality. The people at the club really loved him and he'd bring in small gifts for the girls every now and then.

I learned Sam was born in Poland in 1928. In 1942, he was loaded onto a train bound for Treblinka. Less than two miles from certain death, he jumped from the train and fled into the woods. He was the only one of his family to survive the Holocaust, and subsequently moved to America. At the time we met, Sam was running a very successful butcher operation called Master Purveyors.

Sam had a friend he introduced me to, another Jewish guy named Misha. When I asked Misha what he did for a living, he said he was in the "wheel" business. One day I asked Sam, "What's Misha do, sell tires?"

"What makes you ask that?"

"He told me he's in the wheel business and I don't know what that means."

Sam started roaring. "No, Joey. He's not in the wheel business; he's in the *veal* business."

* * *

One of the first things I did when we opened Babbington's was to suggest to Joe that we buy our meats from Sam Solasz. Joe agreed.

I called Sam and he agreed to supply our meats—all top of the line—to us directly at a price that was better than Joe's supplier. Joe was very happy.

Christmas was approaching and Sam called and said he'd like to have his company Christmas party for forty people at Babbington's. He came in and sat down with Joe to work out the details. They planned a menu that included steak, blackened mashed potatoes, salad, and Joe's special strawberry shortcake. There would be an open bar all night, as well as coffee and tea. On the day of the party, Sam sent a truck over with forty-five shell steaks, meaning five were for the Babbington's crew. It promised to be a good party.

That night the food came out right on time. As Sam's people ate, I made rounds of the tables to make sure everything was running smoothly. Suddenly, I heard Sam's heavy accent from behind me as he said, "Joey, what did this guy do to my steaks?"

I felt a lump in my throat and hesitated a couple seconds before I turned around and said, "Is something wrong, Sam? Just let me know what it is and I'll take care of it."

"No, no, Joey, nothing is wrong. I've never had steak this good. I want Joe to tell me his secret so I can use it in my own restaurant."

I said, "I'm sorry, Sammy. I know you're a crazy Jew, but Joe is just as crazy as you are—maybe more so. You can ask him, but I can tell you right now he won't give up his recipe."

Sam didn't ask and that was the end of it.

I developed a great respect for Sam over the years, for who he is and what he's done. A book was recently written featuring Sam, *Food and the City* by Ina Yalof. It was released in May of 2016. It is a tribute that is well-deserved.

At the age of 89, Sam still works eighty hours per week, and Master Purveyors supplies meats to some of the best restaurants in New York City. He's an amazing man.

* * *

THE DONALD

When Joe and I were running Babbington's, we hosted a lot of parties and did outside catering as well. We ended up catering events for Donald Trump. Every time he sold an apartment in one of his buildings, he'd call us to cater a party. Everything had to be top of the line, both food and beverages. He never quibbled over price.

I met Mr. Trump several times at these events. He was cordial and a regular guy each time I saw him. I liked him.

A few years later, our kids gave my wife and me a weekend getaway package for Trump's Taj Mahal in Atlantic City. We checked in and while Babe was unpacking, I went down to the casino to play some live seven-card stud. Talk about bum luck—I couldn't win a hand.

When Babe came down, I gave her a hundred bucks for the slots. She lost that and my problems continued at the poker table. I decided it was time to give it up and go to dinner. My last hand started out good with three eights. I figured I just might be able to recoup some of my money. I didn't improve my hand and a little old lady beat me out with a small straight she caught on the last card. It was definitely time to leave.

While we were driving down I had told Babe, tongue in cheek, that I'd introduce her to Donald Trump. As we were leaving the poker area toward the steakhouse, who did I see a few feet away but Donald Trump? I told Babe to wait and I walked over to Mr. Trump.

"Excuse me, Mr. Trump," I said. "I'm Joe Silvestri, partners with Joe Babbington. I met you at some of the parties we catered for you."

He smiled and extended his hand. "Sure, Joe. What are you up to?"

I waved Babe over as I said, "I just played some poker. I'd like to introduce you to my wife." He shook her hand.

"Where are you going now?" he asked.

"We thought we'd get a steak dinner."

"Come with me," he said.

We went into the steakhouse and Mr. Trump had the *maître d'* summoned. When he arrived Mr. Trump said, "These people are my personal guests. Give them anything they want and it will be on me."

We didn't see Mr. Trump again that weekend, but the way he treated Babe and me that night—so warm and cordial—really impressed me. In my opinion, he's a real classy guy.

* * *

On the morning of November 9, 2017, Joe Babbington called to tell me that Hillary Clinton had formally conceded the presidential election to Donald Trump. Joe was elated and told everyone he called that he'd known Trump would win all the time.

Although I'm not a political junkie, from what I knew of the Clintons, I sure as hell didn't want Hillary in the White House. I thought about all the Hollywood losers who threatened to leave the country if George W. Bush won a second term—I don't think a single one of them left. The same crew and others like them made the same threats if Trump won. I bet nobody left this time either. That's too bad for us.

Prior to Mr. Trump even being sworn in, the liberals started the same crap they did with Ronald Reagan. Only this time they were more vicious. I have confidence Mr. Trump can handle the attacks though.

Before I let go of this, I want to say something about movie tough guy Robert De Niro. He said he wanted to punch Trump in the face. I think Trump would give De

Niro a beating, but Trump is a little younger and it might not be fair. Well, I'm a little older than De Niro and I'd love a chance to take Trump's place against the actor. Age difference or not, I'd give him a New York ass-kicking.

And if the president, whoever it is, ever asked me to do something to serve my country, I'd do it gladly and proudly.

15 : MC EXCHANGE

One night while I was working at Babbington's, my friend Mickey Brown and his younger brother Sal stopped in. I had been friends with their dad for many years and they were wonderful boys. Mickey was quite excited and said he had some good news for me.

Mickey told me he had a very good friend who worked on Wall Street. His name was Frankie. He was highly successful and made lots of money. Frankie called Mickey and told him about a bar in downtown Manhattan that had closed. It was a German bar and restaurant named Volk's, which was an old-fashioned steam table operation, serving hot food such as roast beef, pastrami, and corn beef, but it was best known for its liver hot dogs. Anyway, when the owner passed away, he left the place to his two sons, but one had a drinking problem and the other had a coke issue. They lost the place in short order. Frankie saw it as having a lot of potential. However, he didn't know anything about the bar business and asked Mickey to see if I would be interested in getting involved.

I talked with Frankie and from what he told me, it sounded like it might be a good deal. I called the lady who owned the building and made an appointment to look at the place. I took Joe Babbington with me. It wasn't a very big place, but the location was perfect. It was on Trinity Place at the corner of Church Street and was right across from 61 Broadway. It was a magnet for the stockbrokers when they got out of work at 4 p.m. and wanted to have a few drinks and a hot sandwich or liver dog.

Joe and I met with the owner, an old Jewish lady, at the location. One of the first things she said was she wanted $100,000 "key money," which was basically a payoff that would have gone straight into the landlady's pocket.

I said we wanted to look the building over before agreeing to anything. Joe and I took a tour of the place, including the upstairs and basement. In general, it was in ill repair and the basement was such a horror, I was tempted to just walk away. But I went back upstairs to talk with the owner and before my ass hit the seat of the chair, she said, "I want to make sure you understand the $100,000 is firm."

I stood up and said, "Thanks for your time, but I'm not interested."

She pleaded, "Please, please sit down and we'll talk some more."

"Ma'am, there's nothing to talk about. This place is shambles and isn't worth $30,000 key money, much less $100,000. Let's go, Joe, I've got another appointment."

Again, she pleaded with me to sit down. After a few seconds, I relented, and we started to negotiate. After we went back and forth for a few minutes, she said she wanted $50,000 key money and another $27,000 for three months of rent up front. I came back with $30,000 and no rent for the first six months while we completed the renovations, and the place was ready to open. She agreed, and Mickey, Frankie, Joe Babbington, and I became partners in what would become the MC Exchange (*M* for Mickey's mother

Mary; *C* for Frankie's mother Concetta; and *Exchange* for our location).

* * *

We took possession in January 1993 and were making good progress on the renovations until Friday, February 26th. That was the date of the first attack on the World Trade Center (WTC) by radical Islamic terrorists. It was a day six people were killed and over one thousand were injured. It was a day I'll never forget.

That morning, my contractor Mike and I had to go to the Bowery to pick up a new hamburger grill. It was around lunch time when we were on our way back, so we decided to pick up some lunch for the crew working on the renovations. We were headed back with the food at around 12:30, when traffic came to a near standstill. Sirens were wailing as firetrucks, police cars, and ambulances wended their way past the stopped vehicles. It was obvious something serious had taken place.

We finally crept our way to Church Street and it was completely blocked off. The only way we could get past the jam was to go the wrong way down a one-way street. We made it back, unloaded the grill, and went inside. That's when we found out what had happened at the WTC.

Mike and I went outside and started walking in the direction of the WTC. As we got closer, there was debris all over the place, and people covered with soot and dazed expressions on their faces walked past us in the other direction. I won't ever forget those faces. Some of them tried to get into the cabs stuck in the traffic, but the cabbies wouldn't let them in. It was hard for me to believe what I was seeing.

I said to Mike, "We can't do anything here. Let's go back."

It was freezing cold, but I left the door open in case any of those fleeing the scene wanted to come inside for a few minutes to get warm. Some did come in to get out of the cold or use the bathroom. They also wanted to wash their soot-covered faces. Because we weren't open for business yet, the only towels we had were the paper towels the workers used, but they worked. Several of them hugged each other, and many cried. It was very sad, and my heart was broken.

How could this happen in America? Little did any of us know that terrorists would return eight years later to finish the job. The next time, their weapons would be airplanes instead of a truck bomb. When we closed shop for the day, getting out of that area was another nightmare. It took me over two hours to get home.

I'm very patriotic and love my country. In the ensuing days, I developed a deep hatred for the murderers and their attack on America.

* * *

We got our liquor license on May 1, 1993. After a small, private grand opening party, we were ready for business. I quickly found out Wall Street people wanted to get everything for nothing. I started out providing free food, figuring it'd make a big profit on the bar business. It went okay for a while, but those people weren't drinking like I thought they would—they were eating well though. My overhead was too high to continue like that and I knew I had to make a move, even if it meant splitting with Joe Babbington.

I'd become friends with a hedge fund guy, and one night he came up and threw me a lifeline. He said, "I know two gorgeous girls, who are very good friends of mine. They're working on Nassau Street and their boss is really abusing them. I think if you put a couple of girls in here, you'd do well."

I'd thought about that earlier. And now that I was seeing the kind of money I *wasn't* making, I figured it was worth a shot. And that was how I met Georgette and Anka. They were Rumanian sisters and absolutely drop-dead gorgeous. When we had our first meeting, I was impressed with their looks and personalities and I'll always remember what they told me: "We never fuck the boss." They turned out to be two of the best bartenders I'd seen in a very long time. Our friendships have lasted from 1993 until today.

At the time, we were open from eleven until around seven or so to catch the after-work crowd—the same guys who were eating me out of house and home. When Georgette and Anka started to work, that changed. The eaters became good drinkers and it wasn't long before I was pushing more Budweiser than any other joint in the area. My distributor fixed me up with special deals like two-for-ones and free hats and t-shirts. The seven o'clock closing time became a thing of the past and we were jammed from the closing bell on Wall Street until midnight most nights. In addition to Budweiser, I struck pay dirt with a drink called Jägermeister. It packed quite a wallop at 70 proof. My clientele loved downing shots and beers. We were the hottest show in town. The girls took care of me and my business, and I took care of them.

I was so happy with Georgette and Anka that I asked them if they knew a couple more girls they could bring on board. They brought in their cousin Stephanie, who was even more beautiful than either Georgette or Anka, and another knockout named Jessie. Jessie wasn't the brightest bulb, but she had all the features and knew how to use them.

My final story about the MC Exchange is from June 1994, when the New York Rangers snapped a 54-year drought and won the Stanley Cup. That celebration was one for the books. They had a big parade with floats and the whole nine yards. I didn't know the girls knew the Rangers players, but there they were on rollerblades, with MC Exchange t-shirts, getting hoisted onto a float with the players. After the parade, we were standing room only until we closed around two the next morning. It was insane.

It was great, but it was again time for me to move on.

16 : THE MORTGAGE BUSINESS

In around late 1994, I rejoined Joe Babbington and we moved Babbington's out of Chelsea to a location on 95th Street, between Columbus Avenue and Central Park West. It was a real nice step-down restaurant with a good kitchen, a small office in the back, and a seating capacity of nearly eighty. We didn't have to put much money into the place— an interior coat of paint and a new outside awning to change the look of the place. The only problem was we didn't have our liquor license right away, but we made up for it with a good food business.

When we did get our booze license, I thought it was a bad thing because we lost our older customers and drew a younger crowd—groupies, hippies, whatever you wanted to call them. I'm not saying they were all bad, but I liked our original clientele much better.

I started doing promotions and brought in a group led by one of the best jazz guitarists in all of New York City, if not beyond. His name was Joe Puma. He was an absolutely amazing talent. He once cut an album with one of my favorite singers, Morgana King—what a voice she had. She was also an actress and played Mama Corleone in *The Godfather*.

I'd grown tired of the restaurant business, however, and told Joe I was going to try some other things. I said if he ever needed me to help out, he'd only have to call and I'd be there. With that understanding, I left Babbington's and was soon working with a mortgage company.

Two very smart young men, Mark Pellettieri and Josh Weiner, got me into the business. I had known Mark's father for years—he was a very sharp and loyal guy. Although we weren't blood relatives, Mark called me Uncle Joe as a sign of respect.

Mark called me one day and asked if I'd meet him and Josh at their office. As I pulled up in front, I saw a crew installing a big new front window. Mark and Josh came outside to meet me. Mark said, "We need to talk, Uncle Joe, but we don't want to do it inside."

We made small talk for a couple of minutes, then they explained the banks weren't doing much business with *C* and *D* papers (poor credit scores); they were mainly handling *A* credit paper (high FICO scores). The company they worked for catered to *C* and *D* applicants who found it very difficult to get a mortgage through the banks, and there was serious money to be made.

Mark then said he and Josh had been working for two other young guys who ran a larger business with several brokers working for them. The trouble was that the other guys were shorting them on their commissions. They were beat artists and thought they were tough guys, so they just withheld the money. When Mark and Josh realized what was going on, they left the company to open their own business.

A few days after they'd left to open their own company, their former bosses showed up at Mark and Josh's new location with three other goons they'd never seen before.

Words were exchanged and one of the three thugs smashed a computer to the floor while another threw a chair through the front window. Before leaving, a threat was issued not to open the business. Concerned, Mark told Josh he was going to call me for advice.

When Mark finished his explaining, I asked, "The only reason you left those guys is because they were cheating you on your commissions?"

"That's right, Uncle Joe," Mark said. "That's the only reason."

"Okay. I don't want to get into this and get embarrassed. You didn't do anything wrong when you were with them?"

"We're being totally honest with you, Uncle Joe. We didn't do anything wrong. I swear on my mother."

That was good enough for me. "One of those guys has an uncle who is a VIP, is that right?"

"That's what I understand, but I don't know his name," Mark said.

"Don't worry about that, I can find out if I have to. Now, tell me more about those guys. Are they gamblers or druggies? What do these clowns do when they're not working?"

"They're both in their thirties and they're potheads. On weekends they buy bags of pot and take it to their boat and get stoned. They never leave the pier."

"Here's what I want you to do. Call them and tell them you want them to meet your Uncle Joe at Babbington's Restaurant tomorrow night around eight. And tell them not to be late."

The next day, I made some inquiries about one guy's uncle. It turned out I'd known him for years. He was a fair and decent man, and I'd be able to talk with him if it became necessary.

Mark and Josh picked me up that evening and we drove to Babbington's. I told Joe I was expecting a couple guys for a meeting. When they showed up, there were four, not two. I asked the other guys who they were. "We're with them," one said, nodding toward the potheads who had taken seats at our table.

"Okay. But you're not part of this meeting and you're not sitting with us. If you want to stay, you're going to sit over there," I said, pointing to a table several feet away. "And keep your mouths shut." They did as told.

I turned to Frick and Frack and said, "I understand you came to my office, wrecked my new computer, and smashed out my window. Is that correct?"

No answer.

"You also said we shouldn't open up. Is that correct?"

No answer.

"Let me spell it out for you. You owe me a new computer and the cost of replacing that window. You can agree right now and it will end here, unless you have something to tell me."

Frick whined, "We were upset because they left without giving us two weeks' notice and they took a couple of accounts with them."

I looked at Mark and Josh. "Is that true? Did you steal accounts?"

Mark said, "No, Uncle Joe. We left with two accounts that were ours. Josh and I brought them in and we never got our commissions on them."

I turned back to Frick and Frack. "Let's talk about commissions. Mark and Josh said you beat them out of their commissions. What do you say about that?"

Frick again answered. "We didn't beat them, the bank beat us. We couldn't pay them money we didn't get."

"I've heard enough," I said. I turned my attention to Frack. "I know your uncle very well. If we don't resolve this tonight, we'll discuss it with him and I'll put all my cards on the table. I know you two like to go on your boat on weekends and I know what you do there. It doesn't make any difference to me, but I don't know what your uncle thinks about it. If we have to meet with him, if you don't tell him, I will."

Frick said, "Tell us again what we have to do to get this over with."

"Very simple. Get me a new computer and pay for the window. Get the price of the window from Mark and Josh. And I want to be up and running by tomorrow. Agreed?"

They both said yes.

After they left, Mark said, "Uncle Joe, you didn't even offer them a cup of coffee."

I said, "Remember one thing: you never break bread with the enemy."

Mark and Josh did the right thing and offered me a job. I didn't know much about the mortgage business or C and D papers, but the boys were good teachers and I learned fast. I put out some calls to let people know where I was. One of my first calls was to Richie Alfaro at Old Riverhead Motors. As soon as he found out what I was doing, he wanted to know if I could get him a commercial loan. I got all the information and ran it past Mark and Josh. They said no problem.

I said, "I appreciate this. I want to make sure you understand Richie is a personal friend of mine—I've known him almost fifty years. Make your earn, but don't hurt this guy. And don't let the bank bullshit him with points on the end and points on the front. Make your commission but treat him right."

They assured me they would. That was my first account and I didn't even have my feet wet yet. Everything seemed to be going well and I was really enjoying myself.

Our office was in Forest Hills, just a few minutes from my house, and not far from where my dear friend Tony "Nap" Napoli lived. Tony loves to walk, and he'd frequently stop at my office and spend some time chatting with me. Things turned around when the commission for Richie's loan came through though. Mark and Josh were still using the bank from the old place and we got shorted.

I asked them, "Why are you still doing business with that bank?"

"Uncle Joe, we don't have another bank."

"Don't put anything else in with them. I'm going to do something about this."

I didn't know anything about the banking business, but I was determined that we weren't going to continue to get robbed.

My granddaughter Vanessa was dating a young man named Anthony, who worked for a big mortgage company called Ideal Bank & Mortgage. I called Vanessa and asked if it would be okay if I spoke with him. She said it wouldn't be a problem and I should give him a call. I reached out to him and invited him over to my office. He liked the place and our operation.

At that time, my wife and I were living upstairs in our house, and Vanessa and her mother lived downstairs. A couple of days after Anthony visited my office, he came to our house for dinner. After the meal, I invited him outside to talk. I asked him if it would be possible for me to meet his boss, Sam Barretta. Anthony said he didn't foresee a problem and he'd set up an appointment for me. Two days later, I met Sam in his office.

Sam wasn't a big man, but he had a big smile, a big personality, and a big brain. I explained our operation to him and how well we were doing with the *C* and *D* papers. He said, "That sounds very interesting. I'd like to come over and see your place."

He came over a few days later, met Mark and Josh, and was impressed by what he saw. He asked us to come to his office the next morning at ten. When we met, we were blown away. He wanted us to become a part of his firm, and they were doing some things in the building and might be able to make room for us there. Not long afterward, we moved into the Ideal Bank & Mortgage building at One Carle Place. If I may say, it was an *ideal* situation. We made a lot of money for Sam and ourselves.

* * *

During another of Tony Nap's visits to my office, he told me about a guy he knew who might be somebody I could do business with. Tony said his name was Frank Cioli. He was very wealthy, with a ton of real estate holdings of different kinds—buildings, commercial properties, and businesses—including a marina on City Island in the Bronx, a health spa in Hunter Mountain, a construction company, and a pizza joint called Grimaldi's, located at 17 Old Fulton Street.

What caught my eye was the marina and Grimaldi's. The marina was of interest because Josh had recently met a guy who had a product for marinas. I thought it might be something this Frank Cioli would be interested in, so I asked Tony to call and ask him to stop in and see me. He was there the next day. I pitched the guy with the marina product to him, but he wasn't interested.

Afterward, we went for coffee. We made some small talk, then Frank asked if I could help him get a mortgage on one of his buildings in Brooklyn. I asked him how his credit was and he said it was in the sixes, which put him in line for a sub-prime loan. I told him I'd run it by Mark and Josh and get back to him. We got him the mortgage and everybody was happy.

Through our affiliation with Sam Barretta, we had access to a daily list of all foreclosures nationwide. Foreclosures were an amazing tool for C and D papers, so every day I browsed that list for anything local. One morning, I found a house in Malba, Queens, that had been foreclosed on. That was a rarity in itself, and it was only $32,000. Some of the better known former residents of Malba included George Burns and Gracie Allen, and Fatty Arbuckle and Clara Bowe, and home prices there ran in the millions. Something wasn't kosher. I told Mark and Josh about it and said I was going to drive out and take a look. When I got to the address, I thought the exterior didn't look that bad. However, compared to the beautiful homes around it, I could see how it could be in foreclosure.

I walked up the three stone steps to the front door, rang the bell, and walked back down. I did that because I knew from previous experience, you never knew what to expect when you knocked on a stranger's door. I'd been attacked once before by a guy who thought I was a process server, and it wasn't going to happen again.

A sloppily-dressed guy answered the door and asked me what I wanted. I identified myself, stepped up, and gave him my card. I said, "I saw your house on the foreclosure list."

He went nuts. "Foreclosure? That's bullshit, I'm not in foreclosure!"

I said, "It's on the list that you're in foreclosure for $32,000."

"I paid that this morning," he ranted.

I said the payment probably hadn't been posted yet and apologized. He calmed down and then asked me if I could sell his house. I asked how much he wanted for it.

"I want $800,000 firm. No commission payments or other bullshit."

I said, "I make my living on the commissions I earn."

"I don't care. I don't pay commissions."

I didn't argue with him. I told him I'd see what I could do and left. When I got back to the office, I called Frank and told him about the house. He said, "Okay, Joe, go ahead and make the deal." Just like that, based on my phone call, sight unseen.

The next morning, I was back in Malba. The same guy answered the door, wearing the same outfit, with a cigarette hanging out of his mouth, looking like he just didn't belong in that neighborhood.

I said, "Good news. I got the $800,000 for you."

"No good," he said.

"What do you mean?"

"My neighbor offered me $825,000."

I knew that was a lie but there wasn't much I could do about it. "So if I can match that, we've got a deal?"

"That's right. Just remember I don't pay commissions."

I went back to the office and called Frank. He said, "Don't worry about it. Go back and make the deal."

Back to Malba I went. "We're all set. I got you the $825,000."

"No good. My wife wants $850,000."

"You said you wanted $800,000 and I got it for you. Then you said you wanted $825,000 and I got it for you. Now you're telling me you want $850,000?"

"That's right. My wife said she wants $850,000 and that's what I've got to get."

To say I was annoyed would be the understatement of the year. Back in the office, I called Frank again.

He said, "Joe, I told you not to worry about it. Make the deal."

"But you haven't seen the house yet. I have no idea what it's like inside."

"Joe, I'm telling you to make the deal and not to worry."

The third time was the charm and the owner accepted Frank's offer. I made an appointment for Frank to look at the house the following Thursday. When we got there, Frank looked at the outside and said it looked good. I said, "But you haven't seen the inside yet."

"Joe, look around you. This is Malba. For $850,000, this place is a steal. It's a steal, Joe."

We completed the paperwork and Frank asked for immediate possession. That meant the owner, his wife, and two kids needed a house. It happened that Frank was building six houses near his marina. Four were still under construction, but two were completely finished. Frank sold him both of those houses for $750,000, so the place in Malba only cost him $100,000.

The purchase price of the house was a good deal, but the interior had to be renovated. Frank and I met with the contractor there, and when I left, two Asian guys were outside on the sidewalk. "House for sale? House for sale?" one of them asked.

"Sure, house for sale."

"How much want?"

"How much will you give?

"Two million. We give two million dollars."

Frank could have sold a house for two million that he'd just bought for eight hundred-fifty thousand — incredible. He didn't sell it to them though. He hung onto it and still owns it, as far as I know.

Frank and I became pretty close and he invited me to come to work for him. I was still doing pretty well with Ideal so I said no. When the sub-prime business began to fade about six months later, I accepted Frank's offer. Mark and Josh stayed with the business for a few more months and then they left too.

17 : FRANK CIOLI

When I started working for Frank, I had no idea what my job description was. For the first couple of weeks, I rode around with Frank as he touched base with various people he dealt with. It was good because I got to know who he knew and I met some interesting characters. During that time, I felt Frank was feeling me out—watching how I conducted myself and figuring out where I'd be the most productive.

Frank owned a very big complex in Bay Ridge in Brooklyn and he asked me if I'd mind collecting some rents for him. I said okay, but before I did that, he assigned me to clean out the basement of the building. I wasn't crazy about it, but I knew I had to do it. There was no heat in the basement and it was brutally cold. I was freezing my ass off, making it an even more uncomfortable job.

A couple of weeks later, Frank hired another guy, a real nice man named John Boyle, to work with me (John died about three years ago from Lou Gehrig's disease). Right after that, Frank again asked me if I'd mind collecting some rents. I said I'd do it—no problem. Wrong! It was a big problem because it turned out Frank was a slumlord.

If you don't know what a slumlord is ... simply put, it's someone who owns a building with apartments and maximizes his profits by spending the least amount possible on maintaining the property. These slumlords get low-income tenants through Section 8 of the Housing Act, which allows them to get checks directly from the government agency providing rental assistance. Frank's tenants were Section 8 people.

Anyway, when I knocked on the door of one of the apartments, a guy opened it and behind him, I could see six more adults, and two kids crawling around on the floor in the kitchen. The adults were fully dressed and wearing coats and scarves. The kids had on snow suits. The only heat in the apartment came from a gas oven. I learned later that if oil was selling for a penny more than Frank wanted to pay, he wouldn't buy it, and the tenants didn't have any heat. After seeing the horrible living conditions, I told Frank that rent collecting wasn't for me. He said that was okay and he had something else in mind for me. We went to Grimaldi's and had a pizza. While we were eating, Frank said he wanted me to look at a restaurant up the hill in Brooklyn Heights he was interested in.

The next day, I went to the restaurant and introduced myself to the owner. I told him I was a friend of Frank's and wanted to look around. He was very accommodating. He asked me if I'd like something to eat and had the chef prepare four different pasta dishes for me, all of which were pretty good.

I asked the owner, "Is anybody else involved in the business?"

"What do you mean?"

"Are you connected to any wise guys? Do you owe any money to shylocks?"

"No, it's just me."

"So everything is legit?"

"Definitely, definitely, definitely."

After I left, I met with Frank. I told him my gut feeling was that he should pass on buying the restaurant. I said the main reason was because for some reason, the people in Brooklyn Heights tended not to support local businesses, and without the locals, it would be tough to generate a profit. He listened and then did just the opposite. He wanted to invest his money and he did. About six months later, the restaurant folded. It wasn't because of bad food or service— it was because the locals didn't show up.

After that, I started picking Frank up in the morning and taking him around the city to his meetings with various people. We were sometimes in Brooklyn, the Bronx, and even Westchester County. Some of the people he met with weren't so nice and some were flakes, but Frank was the biggest flake of all.

No matter where we went during the day, we always ended up at Grimaldi's.

* * *

Grimaldi's was an unbelievable business. It was rated the best pizza in New York for ten or twelve years running. Let me tell you how good it was. Lines started forming outside the door at around 11 a.m., growing quickly to seventy-five or a hundred people. We were the second store on the block and as the day went on, the lines grew, stretching past the business next to us, a place named Pete's, to the end of the block. The early crowds were mostly tourists, while the locals and celebrities joined them later in the day and evening. The lines didn't disappear until between 11:30 and midnight. These crowds translated into Grimaldi's doing four million dollars a year in business. That's right: four million dollars a year *selling pizza.*

Amazingly, the place put up those kinds of numbers with almost no outside advertising. Frank got a lot of free promos through the local TV stations, whose reporters frequented Grimaldi's and bragged about it on the air. It was virtually all word of mouth.

Because of the tremendous number of people that lined up, keeping the line orderly and moving smoothly was a priority. Frank knew I had experience running the line at the Copa and before long, he decided to try me out in that capacity at Grimaldi's. Prior to that, a waiter had been handling the line in addition to his inside duties. Frank did it that way because he was too cheap to hire an extra person. That caused hard feelings because the waiters were knocking down a couple of grand a week in tips and didn't want to spend their time outside. My presence tickled the wait staff and I quickly impressed Frank with my talent for handling the line. Not to boast, but I was very good at it. I kept things moving, which was very important when it was brutally cold, and a wait time of an hour and a half wasn't unusual. When it was that cold, I tried to find a way to get the children and elderly in first. The hot weather could be equally tough on anyone waiting outside. To prevent cases of dehydration, I had Frank put a watercooler and ice outside on the sidewalk. The customers appreciated it and I'm sure it helped to avoid heat-related health issues. I enjoyed it, and customers and staff alike were happy.

One of the things I soon noticed was there seemed to be fewer locals in line than I thought there should be. I found out the reason for that was because the locals felt they shouldn't have to stand in line—that was for tourists.

I remedied that when I recognized locals in line, saying to them, "The rest of your party is already inside. Go right in." That pleased them without causing a riot. The locals became a larger percentage of our customers.

Another problem I dealt with was customers who would finish eating, get their check, and then just sit there talking. In those instances, I'd approach them very diplomatically and say, "Excuse me. You have your check and I'd appreciate it if you'd pay it. I have two hundred people waiting outside and I'd like to get them in." Occasionally I'd get an argument, but most of the time, they'd get up and pay their bill.

Pete's restaurant was one of the oldest establishments in the city. During the winter when our line extended in front of his place, he'd have a waiter come out and invite people to come in, have a drink, and get out of the cold. Some people did and ended up eating at Pete's. I didn't care though; we had no shortage of customers.

People tended to like me, and I got along well with my co-workers and the customers. The wife of a well-known doctor commented about me when she was checking out at the cash register, "He's the classiest guy who has ever worked at Grimaldi's." Coming from her, that was quite a statement.

One night, a reporter from Channel 11 wanted to interview me on camera. I agreed to give her fifteen minutes. She showed up with her crew and lights and we did the interview. The reporter said she wanted to review the recording to see if she needed anything else. While that was going on, Lady Gaga came in. When she saw the camera crew, she told the waiter, "I'm not going to be interviewed. *Get that camera crew out of here.*"

The waiter said, "They are here to interview Joe, not you. You don't have anything to worry about." She wasn't happy about that, but I'm glad the waiter told her the truth. I later came to have a lot of respect for her as an entertainer and a person.

Some of the other celebrities who came in were Frank Sinatra's granddaughter, AJ, a wonderful girl. Anybody connected to Sinatra always got in. And Danny DeVito. He's a great guy. Every time he came in, he asked to get the checks for the tables on his left and right. No other Hollywood celebrity ever did that. And his wife, Rhea Perlman, was just as nice.

We had put a small pizza store in a club named Limelight. It was a popular place, but it was a drug den and eventually closed down. One night, I stopped in and when I walked into our pizza shop, Rhea was standing there waiting for a pizza. I told the guy behind the counter to get her order out right away. Then I took her hand and walked her out into the club. Whenever someone recognized her, they would want to take a picture with her. She accommodated them all. When we went back in our store to get her pizza, I showed her the picture of me and Danny we had hanging on the wall.

I said, "There's your pal right there." She really appreciated that photo being on display.

* * *

I mentioned Lady Gaga and Danny DeVito being customers at Grimaldi's, and they were just a couple of the many celebrities from the entertainment industry who dropped in. In addition, there were local media people and politicians. I want to tell you about one of the better-known visitors from the political realm. Her name is Michelle Obama and her visit caused quite a stir.

I don't remember the date, other than it was during her husband's first term. I got a call from Frank that Michelle and her daughters planned to visit the restaurant that afternoon. I knew that kind of thing would be a zoo, so I told him I appreciated the heads up, but unless he really needed me, I'd come in for my regular shift later in the day.

When I got to work, Michelle and the children had just left, so I didn't see her in person, but the staff quickly filled me in on their visit. I had been right; it was quite chaotic. First, the outside line of between one hundred-fifty and two hundred people had to be moved across the street. Traffic was shut down on Fulton so the move could be made. That was followed by several black SUVs pulling up to unload the Obamas and their security people. Foot traffic was limited as well. If you were in one of the other businesses on the block, you had to stay where you were until the Obamas departed. I remember hearing that a guy doing renovation work on a place down the street tried to go to his van to get some tools and was stopped by the Secret Service. The block and its businesses were shut down—nobody got in, nobody got out.

Despite the turmoil, Mrs. Obama received glowing remarks from the staff. They said she was very pretty and gracious.

After the Obamas left, things didn't settle down right away. The people who had been inside the restaurant and those who had been in line were buzzing over the excitement of the visit. And in the days following, we got great coverage in the local media about the First Lady stopping in and her comment that even though she was from Chicago, Grimaldi's pizza was the best she had ever tasted. For the next couple of weeks, the increase in business was dramatic.

* * *

Grimaldi's was a gold mine and I really enjoyed working there. However, Frank Cioli had a dark side that hurt a lot of people. To understand that aspect, I need to begin with the man who owned the business next door to Grimaldi's. His name is Marcello Pevida and his place was called #1 Front Street.

18 : THE REAL FRANK EMERGES

One of the nicest persons I met while working at Grimaldi's was a woman from Australia. Her first name was Lisa, but I don't remember her last name. She was very pretty and highly intelligent.

Lisa was a big shot with the airlines and her job brought her to New York multiple times per year. She heard about Grimaldi's and stopped in one evening. The line was very long, and she approached me. She said she had a party of ten and wondered if they would have to wait, and if so, for how long.

A party of ten is something you don't want to lose. I knew there was a table of twelve that had just finished eating, so I brought Lisa and her friends to that table as soon as it was empty. After that, she stopped in regularly with parties ranging from six to ten. It was always a good time, a big tab for the restaurant, and a big tip for the waiters. So everybody looked forward to her visits.

We became quite close and Lisa started bringing me gifts whenever she was in town. She even gave me a gift for my first great-grandchild. She brought her husband with her a couple of times as well. He was a business agent, and actor Russell Crowe was one of his clients. Lisa loved her pizza and she loved the way I ran Grimaldi's. She always complimented me and shook my hand. She was a classy lady and I had great respect for her.

One day, Lisa asked me what I thought of opening a Grimaldi's in Australia, and running it.

It sounded like a tremendous opportunity, but I didn't jump on it right away. I was concerned about something that happened a few weeks earlier involving a similar deal with Frank. I stalled Lisa by saying I'd have to think about it.

* * *

Marcello Pevida, the operator of #1 Front Street, was a former NYPD cop. On September 11, 2001, he and his partner responded to the World Trade Center terror attacks. A piece of falling debris landed on the trunk of their car, breaking Marcello's spine, leading to him retiring on disability. I found him to be a real man, a hero, and a terrific guy. We became very good friends. The following is his account of that terrible day, as he told it to me. It will help to explain why I hold Marcello in such high regard:

> On September 11, 2001, I was assigned to the 5th Precinct, Squad B2, working the day tour with Detective Billy Malloy. Our patrol area included the World Trade Center (WTC).
>
> At approximately 8:10 a.m., we saw and heard the first hijacked plane crash into Tower One of the WTC. We arrived on the scene within minutes and were the third patrol car to respond. It was obvious that the damage to the building was tremendous and people were already exiting the Tower, some

in a state of panic. After initially going inside, we returned to the street to direct the fleeing workers to safety and make room for rescue workers and ambulances to park.

As we were clearing the area, a second plane crashed into Tower Two. It sounded like an incoming missile and the explosion was thunderous. I was behind the wheel of my patrol car at the time when a large piece of debris, later determined to be a piece of the plane's fuselage, struck the rear of the car, crushing it and jamming the metal cage between the front and back seats into my seat. It resulted in an injury to my back that would eventually end my career in law enforcement. However, due to the adrenaline rush of the moment and shock, I wasn't readily aware of the extent of my injuries.

Getting out of the wrecked car, Billy and I tried to assist the growing number of people attempting to escape from the building. They were all scared and some were injured. We saw a female police officer laying on the sidewalk and bleeding from a wound to her head. As Billy and I were assisting her to her feet, we were showered with falling glass and other debris. We all crawled under a parked truck for safety. We subsequently got her to an Emergency Medical Services unit and asked them to tend to her. Three Emergency Services Unit vehicles arrived on the scene. As I watched them enter the building, I didn't realize it was the last time I'd ever see them alive.

Billy and I were then assigned to help remove the civilians under the bridge connecting Tower One with Building Seven. By this time, the area was like a war zone with falling glass, chairs, and other dangerous objects. But the worst thing was the people. Those trapped on the upper floors with no means of escape were jumping, rather than burn to death. One of the jumpers landed on top of a fireman and both of their bodies literally exploded right before our eyes. The same fate befell the other jumpers when they struck the sidewalk. These were sights no one should ever have to see, and I won't forget them for as long as I live.

When Tower Two collapsed, we were taken by surprise and engulfed by smoke and dust—we were ordered to evacuate and ran for our lives. We got out of the smoke and dust after two blocks, and were attempting to make our way back to the scene through the throngs of fleeing people and debris, when we were again overcome by a white fog as Tower One fell. When we arrived there, only thirteen floors remained. The dead and injured were everywhere. Some were so badly hurt, they didn't want to be touched. I was having a very hard time breathing, and on top of that, none of our radios or phones were working so we had no way of knowing what was going on outside of our immediate area. It was a nightmare.

I worked for three days afterward before my injuries got the better of me. I had to have back surgery and my lungs were damaged for life. I was forced to retire on disability.

As I said, to me, Marcello is a true hero.

* * *

One evening at Grimaldi's, Marcello, who had the nickname of Mars, and I were talking. He said, "Joe, what do you think Frank would say about renting my place? I'd close my restaurant and you guys would have the whole place."

It so happened the lady Frank was leasing from was acting to evict him because he was late with his rent payments and other bills, so I figured Mars' proposal might be a lifeline for him.

I said, "I'll talk with Frank and get back to you."

"Sure, I understand. Have your talk and let me know."

I saw Frank later that evening and told him about my conversation with Mars. He said, "That would be great. Let's set it up."

I drew up a plan and talked it over with Mars. He liked it. I figured Frank would okay it too and we were all set. And then the landlady backed off on the eviction and Frank lost interest. But she soon renewed her efforts and Frank knew he had to make a move. That's when he threw in the monkey wrench. "I'll talk to my son Joseph and see what he thinks."

That bothered me. Joseph was headquartered in Arizona and handled setting up all the Grimaldi's locations in the western United States. However, he had nothing to do with New York—that was Frank's turf. Joseph wasn't my cup of tea and I didn't want him involved.

I said, "This is something you and I can decide. What do you need to talk with Joseph for?"

"This is a major move for us and I want him involved. I *am* going to call him."

I didn't like it, but it was clear Joseph was going to play a role in whatever agreement was reached.

Joseph was in California working on another deal when Frank called him. Frank told me that Joseph jumped on Mars' offer right away and was anxious to meet with him.

I called Mars and told him Frank was interested in his proposal. He said, "That's good news, huh?"

"Good and not so good."

"What do you mean?"

"Frank wants me to arrange a meeting with you, him, and his son Joseph. Because you're a dear friend, I've got to tell you up front that I don't like Joseph. Personally, I wouldn't get in bed with him. Now you're forewarned."

"I appreciate knowing that, Joe. I'll keep that in mind when we meet. Go ahead and set it up."

When Joseph got involved, the deal I originally proposed was scrapped and I was shut out.

Mars and his partner Tom figured that based on the four million dollars the Grimaldi's location made in the small store the previous year, that figure could reach six million with the bigger place and a full liquor license. They worked out the financial arrangements and made their deal.

On opening night, I wasn't there because Frank assigned me to our new location on Coney Island. Thinking I'd manage the store in his building had been one of the selling points when Mars made his offer to Frank. When he asked Frank where I was, Frank said, "I had to assign Joe to Coney Island. That place is going to end up being one of our best locations."

Getting shut out of Mars' location wasn't the end of it, however. There was more to come.

* * *

After the New York operation was up and running, Mars approached me with another idea. He said, "We've got an Asian restaurant in the Hard Rock Hotel in Fort Lauderdale. The place isn't making any money and I'm wondering if we could put a Grimaldi's in there. Are you interested in that?"

"Yeah, that sounds like a good idea. I'll talk it over with Frank."

When I mentioned it to Frank, he liked it but said he'd have to bring Joseph into it. What the fuck? First with the New York deal and now again with Florida. I said, "Why? This is just between you and me."

Frank shook his head. "There's gambling there, Joe. I've got to bring my son in on this."

I again protested. "We'll be running a pizza joint. We won't have anything to do with the gambling."

"Maybe not, but just the same, I'm making that call."

That was the end of the discussion. Joseph was going to be in and I knew that meant I'd be shut out again. And I was.

I told Marcello that Frank was interested, and that Joseph would be part of the deal. I repeated my warnings about Joseph. Despite that, a meeting was set up that included Frank, Joseph, Mars, his partner Tom, and his close friend Chris. I learned later I wasn't invited because Joseph didn't want me there.

After the meeting, Joseph was supposed to go back out west. He circumvented that plan, and instead went to Fort Lauderdale to speak with the owner of the Hard Rock, who was friends with Mars and Tom. Joseph introduced himself as the owner of Grimaldi's and said he was there to finalize arrangements for the move to the Hard Rock.

The owner said, "I've been dealing with Mars."

Joseph responded, "From now on, you're dealing with me. Forget about Mars."

After Joseph left, the owner called Mars and told him what happened. Mars told me, and I said he needed to talk with Frank. When he did, Frank denied having any knowledge about what Joseph had done.

Did I want to get involved with Lisa and her idea for a Grimaldi's in Australia? Under these circumstances, not on your life.

* * *

The relationship between Mars and Frank went downhill quickly. Frank stopped paying Mars the rent for #1 Front Street. When Mars took him to court, Frank told the judge he couldn't afford the $20,000 per month, but he would pay $900 per day. If you do the math, that amounts to $27,000 per month. But Frank's logic was that he'd pay a couple of days and then skip a couple of days, pay a couple more days, and then miss a couple. Mars and Frank were always in and out of court.

On top of that, Mars gave Frank a large sum of money, I think it was three or four hundred thousand dollars, for a stock that Frank was heavily involved with. Frank signed a promissory note on a half sheet of paper he tore from a yellow legal pad. Naturally, Frank reneged on the deal and never paid Mars back.

Frank has an ego as big as all outdoors and he sells everybody short.

* * *

One day, Frank told Mars they should meet and resolve their differences. A meeting was arranged, and Mars asked me to attend as his witness to what was said. Frank showed up with the two jerkoffs he usually had with him. Mars came in a few minutes later. I wish I'd have gone outside and waited for Mars. I'd have suggested he not go to the meeting. But I didn't, and it was what it was.

Anyway, Frank went into a spiel about how he wanted to start over with Mars and go back to their original deal. They'd shake hands and be friends again.

Mars said he liked the idea but reminded Frank that he hadn't kept his word the first time. Frank said this time would be different. They shook hands.

And then Frank said, "On Friday, I'll give you the million I promised you as part of our original agreement."

That meeting was on a Tuesday, and Mars called me on Thursday. He said, "You aren't going to believe what happened. Frank's lawyer called my lawyer. He told him that Frank was negotiating with the landlord of #1 Front Street to take over the whole building and I would be out." What Joseph had done to Mars in Fort Lauderdale, Frank was now doing to him in New York.

A couple of months later, Mars asked to meet me at the Coney Island location I was managing. We found a quiet spot outside and talked.

Mars asked, "Joe, do you have anything against me personally?"

"No. Why?"

"Well, Frank told me that you want to come after me physically and he's holding you back."

"I don't have anything against you. I like you a lot and respect you. You're a hero to me. I never said anything about coming after you. Besides, if I did want to hurt you, do you think I'd tell Frank about it? I wouldn't send a letter."

"I didn't think so, Joe. Let's forget about it."

Talk about bullshit. What bothered me the most was that although Mars was retired on disability, he still carried a pistol. Suppose he was a different guy and decided if I planned to come after him, he'd get me first? It gave me something to think about.

After seeing what Frank did to Mars and others, and what he had done to me, it was obvious what he really is: a total hypocrite. He always had a three-month romance with the people he did business with. But after that, he screwed thcm six ways from Sunday. He got his new partners to put up all the money for his various ventures with a promise to pay them back. But he never did, and ended up taking over the businesses. He did that to four people I know of. I have no respect for him as a man.

19 : LAWSUITS

Frank and I parted company, but I had one more dealing with him. Mars sued Frank over the issues concerning #1 Front Street, and Frank decided to file suits of his own. In one of them, he named me as a defendant along with Mars and his partner Tom.

To my surprise, I was contacted by a lawyer who had represented Frank for seventeen years. He said Frank had stiffed him on a bill of $850,000 and was no longer his client. He had heard about our case and wanted to represent me pro bono. I welcomed his offer. He eventually got me removed as a defendant. During that time, we used to talk almost every day. And then suddenly, he stopped calling. I told Mars something was wrong, and it was.

On the day we went to court and the case against me was dismissed, Frank approached me and offered his hand. I told him, "Get the fuck away from me, you bastard."

Right afterward, the attorney and Frank went into a conference room together. It turned out he had gone back to work for Frank. I don't know what Frank offered him or if he'll ever collect. I find it amazing, however, what money, or the promise of money, can do to people.

Mars' lawsuit against Frank has been ongoing for three years and remains unresolved.

Frank has wreaked havoc on many people, including me. I can only hope that someday justice will be served.

EPILOGUE

As I complete this writing, I have just turned eighty-six years old. What I have written has brought back a flood of memories. Some were bad, but most were good. Personally, I'm a sports guy and boxing is my favorite sport. The truly great fighters are successful in large part because they can take a punch. And if they get knocked down, they get back on their feet and continue the fight. That has always been my philosophy. If I get a tough break, I don't let it keep me down: I get up and get back in the fight. So when it comes to regrets, I'm in tune with what Frank Sinatra said in his song "My Way"—"Regrets, I've had a few, but then again, too few to mention."

I do have something I want to get off my chest though. It's been haunting me for sixty-one years and I want to make sure the record is corrected. I'm talking about the fight between the Yankees players and a group of drunken bowlers that took place at the Copa on May 16, 1957 (see Chapter 6). It isn't the fight I regret; it's that Hank Bauer took the weight for something *I* did. Hank has been maligned all these years for a punch I threw. He wasn't even there.

I apologize to Hank's family and friends for that injustice.

Billy Martin was maligned as well. Instead of giving him credit for initially trying to keep the peace that night, the Yankees were looking for a reason to get rid of him and the fight was it. The whole thing was a sad situation for all involved.

I also feel bad for Mars (Marcello) as his case against Frank drags on. He is a great guy and deserves justice. Hopefully it will come soon.

On the plus side, I've had a lot of good things happen to me. Working at the Copa was an exceptional opportunity for me to meet people and learn a lot of things. The health club was another great chance for me to meet celebrities and business people, some of whom offered me jobs.

Most important of all are friends and family. I have many close friends, and Tony Nap is among the closest. He's a guy with a lot of class and a true gentleman. If not for him, this book probably would never have been written.

I also want to acknowledge the Mickey Brown family and Ray Randazzo. They are very near and dear to me. Although Mickey has passed away, his sons Mickey Jr. and Sal are like my adopted children. They are highly successful businessmen and I'm very proud of them. And Mickey's widow is a wonderful woman. Although I don't see her as often as I used to, a true friend is a true friend.

And I've been blessed with a family that is truly priceless. From my dear wife Babe to my siblings, children, grandchildren and now great-grandchildren (the icing on the cake), they are loving and caring, and I adore each and every one of them.

In closing, let me say that even at my age (I don't buy green bananas anymore), I have a couple irons in the fire. If things work out, I'll be back in the restaurant business. That would make me extremely happy, and with a family like mine behind me, why not?

Getting back to Frank Sinatra. The last song he sang when he retired for good was "The Best Is Yet To Come."

My sentiments exactly.

INDEX

A

B

C

D

For More News About Dennis Griffin,
Signup For Our Newsletter:

http://wbp.bz/newsletter

Word-of-mouth is critical to an author's long-term success. If you appreciated this book please leave a review on the Amazon sales page:

http://wbp.bz/afba

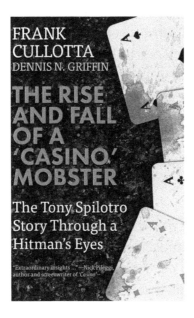
1

A Rocky Start

I'll never forget the first time I met Tony Spilotro. I was just a kid, twelve or thirteen, and I hated school. I was always in trouble with the teachers, and my mother had her hands full trying to get me into a school that could handle me. I loved to fight, too, which caused her even more grief.

Anyway, to hustle up some pocket money I started shining shoes up and down Grand Avenue. One day I noticed a kid about my age shining shoes on the opposite side of the street. He saw me at the same time, and we glared at each other for several seconds.

The other kid hollered to me, "What the fuck are you lookin' at?"

"I'm looking at you. What about it?"

We started walking toward each other, met in the middle of the street, and put down our shine boxes.

He said, "This is my fuckin' territory, and I don't want you on this street. Understand?"

He was short but looked pretty solid, and I figured he could probably take care of himself. That didn't bother me, though, because, like I said, I was a scrapper myself. "I don't see your name on any street signs, and I'm not leaving."

We shoved each other a little bit, but no punches were thrown. Then he said, "I'm coming back here tomorrow, and if I see you, we'll have to fight."

"Then that's what we'll have to do."

I went to that location the next day, but the other kid wasn't there. In fact, it was about a week later when we met again on the street. This time his attitude was different—he wasn't combative. He said, "I've been asking around about you. What's your last name?"

"Cullotta."

"Was your father Joe Cullotta?"

"Yeah. So what?"

"Your father and my father were friends. Your old man helped my old man out of a bad spot one time." He told me his name was Tony Spilotro and his father ran a well-known Italian restaurant on the east side called Patsy's.

I remembered hearing about the incident Tony was talking about. My father (who had been a gangster) liked Patsy and was a regular customer at the restaurant. Back then there was a gang called the Black Hand. It consisted of Sicilian and Italian gangsters who extorted money from their own kind, and my father hated them with a passion. Their method was to shake down business owners by demanding money in return for letting the business stay open. They were making Patsy pay dues every week. When my father heard about it, he and his crew hid in the back room of the restaurant until the Black Handers came in for their payoff. Then they burst out and killed them. After that Patsy wasn't bothered anymore.

From that day Tony and I became friends and started hanging around together. I found out he was a few months older than me, and we had some other things in common besides age and being short. We both hated school and would fight at the drop of a hat.

On weekends I'd see Tony at Riis Park, where he hung out. The first time I went there this guy, who was probably in his twenties, dressed in a shirt and tie and looking like a wiseguy, walked up to me and said, "I'll give you five dollars if you fight my brother."

"Who's your brother?"

He pointed to Tony. "Tony, he's right there."

I laughed. "No, I already had a beef with him. We're friends now."

"Oh, you must be Cullotta. Tony told me about you. I'm Vic Spilotro."

I went over with Tony. A little later Vic came over and said he'd found a kid for Tony to fight. Tony beat the hell out of the kid, and then Vic paid him the five bucks. Tony said, "Hey, what about me? I did all the work. Don't I get anything?"

Vic laughed. "Not you, you're not getting shit. I'm doing this to toughen you up, not so you can make money."

We messed around for a while longer, and then Tony said, "Come with me, and I'll show you where I live. It's right off Grand Avenue."

On the way to his house Tony told me he had five brothers. Vince was the oldest, followed by Vic and Patrick. And then came Tony and his two younger brothers, Johnny and Michael.

Tony showed me through the house. All the boys slept in one bedroom with three sets of bunk beds. While we were in the bedroom Tony's mother walked in. She was a very tiny lady, and I had the impression she wasn't very happy about me being there. She asked who I was, and I told her. If she knew about my father and the Black Hand thing, it didn't seem to make any difference. I still sensed she didn't like me. She said to Tony, "Hurry up and get out of here, the both of you."

After she left I said to Tony, "I don't think your mother likes me and probably doesn't want me around."

He laughed. "Don't worry about it. She doesn't like any of my friends. If she had her way I'd only hang around with altar boys."

As we walked out of the house Tony's mother and father were in the kitchen. Tony said something to them, but neither of them spoke to me. My name wasn't mentioned, and I don't think the father even looked at me as I passed by. Over time I got to know Tony's parents better. They were hard working, nice people. I never knew either of them to be involved in anything illegal.

After that initial meeting I didn't see much of Tony during the week because of school. But on weekends I'd catch up with him at Riis Park. I saw Vic quite a bit, too, at Riis or on the streets. I became convinced he was a gangster because of the way he dressed and that he always had a big wad of money with him. At the time I didn't really understand what it meant to be a bookie, but I'd see Vic getting slips of paper and money from people. I found out later that he was taking sports bets and his operation was backed by the Outfit. He used to run crap (dice) games, too, in the alleys behind the houses in the neighborhood. Although Tony and I were just kids, sometimes Vic let us in the games. Even then, it was obvious to me that Tony was in his element when he could bet on something.

Another guy I met hanging around with Tony was Joey Hansen. Next to me, he probably came to know Tony as well as anybody. He was jealous of my relationship with Tony, and we had a couple of fights over it. I mention him here because he played a role in some of the incidents I'll tell you about later.

Did I know then what the future held for Tony? No, I didn't. But looking back, it's my opinion that Vic Spilotro was the person most instrumental in Tony taking to the criminal life and becoming an Outfit guy. Tony idolized Vic and his lifestyle. Vic introduced Tony to a lot of his associates as he was growing up—more guys with nice clothes, women, and money. And what may have been even more important: power.

* * *

About a year after first meeting Tony we started spending more time together. The reason for that was we both got placed in the same facility—Montefiore School. It was a place that provided educational services for troublemakers—kids who couldn't get along anywhere else. I was sent there first, and Tony showed up about a week later. I don't think he was into criminal stuff then. But like me, he was a kid that most teachers couldn't control.

The student body of Montefiore was primarily black. (We called them "colored" at that time.) Tony and I were two of the half-dozen or so white kids in the place and were constantly in physical confrontations with the blacks. Another thing we didn't like was having to use public transportation to get to and from the school. We couldn't do much about the blacks, but I figured out how to take care of the other.

I'd already learned how to hotwire my mother's car. I started using that knowledge to steal cars from around my neighborhood. I drove the hot car to school and parked it a couple of blocks away. After school I'd drop Tony off at his father's restaurant, where he worked every day, and then I'd drive it back to my neighborhood. Having our own transportation was nice, but it didn't stop the fighting inside the school.

One day when I came out of wood shop I found Tony in the hallway surrounded by four or five blacks. One of them wanted to fight him alone. "Come on, white boy," he said, "just you and me."

Tony agreed. The black kid picked him up and flung him over his head to the floor. Tony got up and put a beating on the guy. Then one of the other blacks said, "Let's kill that white motherfucker," and they started to attack.

I grabbed one of the long poles with a hook on the end that was used to open and close the upper windows. I swung it at the blacks and caught a couple of them in the head, and then Tony and I ran out of the building.

When Tony told Vic what was going on with the blacks, Vic said it was time we taught them a lesson by going after their leader—a kid named Jackson—and he'd go with us.

A few days later Tony and I didn't go to classes, and Vic drove us to the school in his four-door Mercury. We got there at lunch time when we knew all the students would be in the cafeteria. Vic brought along a .45-caliber pistol.

Vic crashed the car through the gates of the fenced-in playground and parked it near the cafeteria. Tony took the gun, and he and I ran inside and grabbed Jackson out of his seat at the lunch table. As we dragged him outside to the car he was scared to death, crying, and screaming. The other blacks were shocked. They followed us outside but didn't do anything. We drove away, pistol-whipped Jackson, and then drove back to the school and dumped him off.

Tony said he wasn't going to go back to school. His father didn't want him to and said he needed him at the restaurant. I did go in the next day, and the juvenile officers were waiting for me—they wanted to throw me in jail for the Jackson thing. They wrote me up and told me I couldn't come back to Montefiore. And then they contacted my mother and said we had to appear before a juvenile court judge.

Tony got charged, too, but his lawyer told the judge that Tony worked at his father's restaurant and any action against him would cause a hardship on his family. It worked, and Tony was released to work at the restaurant. I wasn't as lucky and got placed in a reformatory for six months.

After I got out, I got into more trouble and drew nine months in another reformatory called St. Charles. So I didn't see much of Tony again until we were seventeen or so. We would run into one another from time to time and catch up on the latest happenings in the neighborhood. By that time he was making quite a name for himself as a tough guy and a thief. People already respected and feared him.

Just before Tony turned eighteen we talked about the Outfit. I'll never forget his words to me at that time: "Frankie, I'm going to become one of them. Someday I'm going to be a boss, and I'll take you with me."

At that time I didn't want anyone to run my life for me. I said, "I'm not interested in becoming a gangster."

After that we kind of went our separate ways. I was content with being a thief and running my own crew. Tony was pursuing his ambitions of becoming a member of the Outfit, and I heard he was hooked up with some big time gangsters out of Cicero.

And then one day, about a year and a half later, Tony stopped in to see me. He said he and some other guys had a big job coming up with a lot of money to be made. They were short a man, and he offered me the spot. I immediately said I was in. It was then I learned we were going to take down a bank.

http://wbp.bz/mobstera

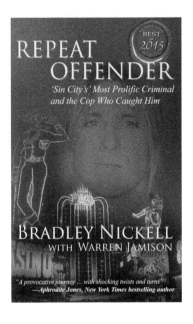
1

In Danger
Just as courage is the danger of life, so is fear its safeguard.
—Leonardo da Vinci

Early one evening, I left the Detective Bureau and soon noticed the same compact car had been in my mirror for a few blocks. A silver colored Toyota, beat-up looking with no front license plate, driven by two Hispanic-looking men. I wasn't sure if they were following me, but I didn't want to take a chance. My nerves were shot. I'd been dreading this exact thing for weeks.

A quick turn down a side street didn't lose them. Maybe if I stopped, they'd pass, but that would've made me an easy drive-by target and I was outnumbered.

I hastily formed my plan. If they continued to follow, I'd phone for patrol units to pull them over as I led them around aimlessly. A call over the police radio might tip them off, though, if they had a scanner.

I hoped a quick jaunt on the freeway might lose them, but they were still there, just a few cars behind, in the lane to my right. The rush-hour traffic slowed. Something ahead was bringing traffic to a complete stop. If these guys were assassins, this might be their best chance—pull up next to me and unload everything they have. The tactic is used south of the border more often than people in the United States know, and they're usually armed to the teeth.

I was ready. One hand on my pistol in my lap and a pump-action 12-gauge shotgun lying across the seat next to me. The car drew up on my right, and I waited for the smallest of signs. The pistol rested between my legs as I jacked a round into the shotgun's chamber. I could feel my pulse beating in my neck.

The driver rolled his window down and threw out a spent cigarette. His chiseled face, backed with dark, lifeless eyes, reminded me of a shark. I pointed the shotgun directly at him, just out of view below the door frame. Safety off. Finger on the trigger.

Each of the five rounds in the shotgun had nine, .33-caliber projectiles inside, just waiting to tear through the door panel and eliminate the threat.

He had no idea what a bad decision he was about to make. Time seemed to stand still.

Neither the driver nor the passenger had even glanced at me. Traffic started to flow again and the moment was over. I relaxed my grip on the shotgun and holstered my pistol. Before I could reflect, I was on the next freeway exit, contemplating another path home.

My heart raced. I had mixed thoughts: thankful it turned out to be nothing, and disturbed that Daimon had gotten inside my head.

Police work is rarely as you see on TV. Real investigations don't begin and end in an hour. Some take months, or years, to complete. And heart-racing, adrenaline-filled moments are sometimes scarce in the endless days of the work grind. But every now and then, maybe once in a career for some cops, a case comes along that could've been conceived by a Hollywood screenwriter.

Weeks before, Chief Deputy District Attorney Sandy DiGiacomo had called; her tone urgent. "Brad, detectives just told me someone has put a hit out on me."

My heart began to thud heavily. A contract killing is nothing to take lightly, especially for a prosecutor who has made a lot of daunting enemies.

"They asked me where my kids are, and said I might want to get them from school." Her voice shook. "And you'll never guess who the bad guy is."

"No way," I said, knowing exactly what she meant.

"Yep . . . Daimon Monroe."

Sandy and I had been working an investigation involving Daimon, a thief who had probably committed more crimes than anyone I've ever known. Clearly, things had just taken a turn for the worse.

"You do whatever they say," I said, picturing Daimon. At first blush, he seemed harmless, small in stature, dressed like a rock star from the 80s, walking with a tough swagger to counterbalance his effeminate appearance. But he was a vain and dangerously clever man with dead eyes. I had a sick feeling in my stomach. "I'll see if I can find out more and give you a call."

Daimon had been in jail for months waiting to be tried on several cases, but he still had access to the phone, mail, and a network of friends on the outside. I was the lead detective in his criminal affairs. Sandy was prosecuting him as a habitual criminal, which meant if he were convicted, he potentially faced a life sentence.

As a detective in the Las Vegas Repeat Offender Program, or ROP team, I know a court case against one thief doesn't seem particularly noteworthy. Not until someone realizes the criminal is repeatedly committing crimes, do people start to see the effect one criminal has on a vast amount of innocent people. And Daimon was the most devious, calculating, prolific thief Nevada had ever seen, stealing millions of dollars of material goods, destroying livelihoods, threatening lives, and harming those who stumbled into his path.

Knowing what I did about Daimon, Sandy could be in real danger. I began checking the recorded inmate phones from Daimon's housing unit hoping to find him, or another prisoner, talking about anything that might indicate whether the threat was real or simply jailhouse talk. The inmates know the phones are recorded, and yet many still talk about their criminal activities. Most of them are smart enough to at least use coded language, but some don't bother.

Each phone call lasted around ten minutes and then the line is automatically disconnected. Depending on how many inmates are in a particular housing unit, there can be anywhere from a few dozen to a few hundred phone calls per unit, per day. Sorting through the calls to find a particular inmate's activity was like finding needles in a haystack. And listening to the calls takes time, as you have to remain alert and mentally invested in each conversation or important information can slip by unnoticed.

After hours of searching and listening, one series of phone calls caught my attention.

An inmate named Johnny had called a man named Rich. Johnny had a thick, Hispanic accent and spoke in rough street-language, but Rich sounded more formal, refined, probably educated.

"Hey, listen," Johnny said. "There's a hit out on a D.A. here, named DiGiacomo. I leaked it to some dummy, and he leaked it downstairs, thinking it was gonna get him somewhere. The guy trying to get this done is Diamond Holt or something like that."

One of Daimon's alias last names is Hoyt. Johnny must've seen some paperwork. Diamond Holt…Daimon Hoyt.

In another phone call, Johnny sounded panicked and began to whisper, so he couldn't be heard by other inmates. "Things have changed since we last spoke, man. He still wants the hit on the D.A., but now he's talking about some detective, and a Judge Leavitt, too."

Johnny sounded like he'd gotten into something he wanted no part of. He didn't want to snitch, but he couldn't sit by and let the hits go down. So he leaked it, knowing the guy would pass the tip to the cops.

Johnny said Daimon was trying to find someone to do the hits for $10,000 each. He also said Daimon might've made a connection with the Aryan Warriors prison gang, and they might've farmed it out to the Sureños gang in Southern California.

This wasn't just jailhouse talk. This was for real.

"He says his number one is this detective named Nickell."

"I'm gonna have somebody come see you," Rich said.

I stopped the tape and replayed it. *"His number one is this detective named Nickell."* Leaning back in my chair, I clasped my hands behind my head and exhaled. This was a first. As a cop, I've had people threaten me in highly charged, emotional moments, but nobody had ever hatched a real plot to kill me. I was just a cop, doing my job. Daimon was making it personal. I'd worked hard to put the Monroe investigation to rest, but things were far from over. <>

http://wbp.bz/roa

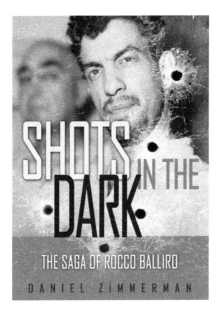

SHOTS IN THE DARK by DANIEL ZIMMERMAN

http://wbp.bz/sitda

Read A Sample Next

Chapter 1

"The Lost"
There he sits in his cell
With nothing left but hope
And then he sees a light beyond
The breaking point of dawn

From somewhere comes a voice of love
To let him know he's not alone
To tell him that he knows the truth
And someday not far away
He'll be free because of you.
(Paula L. Bent, ©1967, Somerville, Mass.)

A sudden gust stirred several lonely leaves, brittle and browned from months of exposure to snow and frost. They tumbled randomly along the edge of the gutter, eventually coming to rest at the base of a rusted chain-link fence which separated adjacent parcels of property. Rugged branches of a huge, leafless oak, witness to more than a hundred such bitter New England winters, groaned under the weight of a thick layer of ice and the pressure of a frigid air mass that had moved in earlier that day.

Heaped waist-high at the leading edge of the sidewalk was a bank of frozen snow, raw evidence of the harsh nor'easter that battered the area several days earlier. It marked the third such punishing storm of the season and the winter of 1963 had yet to reach its midpoint.

On this halcyon night, however, the inky-black skies over Boston were clear. Glinting stars and a suspended half-moon cast a bluish-gray tinge over the snow-covered expanse below.

Standing silent sentry over Centre Street, Roxbury, rows of neatly-trimmed tenement apartment buildings co-mingled with several stately, turn-of-the-century homes. All of the residences were hushed against the post-midnight hour. Most of the occupants had retired early on this particular Friday evening.

That quiet was disturbed by the approach of a motor vehicle, coasting haltingly along the slumbering street. The brake lights burned crimson as the vehicle came to a stop in front of a two-family home. Thick plumes of grayish fog billowed from the tailpipe. The operator cut the headlights. Save for a glimmer of moonlight and scant illumination from several distant streetlamps, the roadway ahead was plunged into darkness.

The apartment interior was entirely devoid of light. The occupants of the automobile attempted to discern any sign of movement from within. There was nothing. The dwelling seemed vacant. Could the darkness be intentional? Were there occupants who preferred not to be seen?

After a moment, the car moved forward, turned right on Cedar Street, and came to a stop adjacent to the snow-shrouded sidewalk. In the distance, lights from the city of Boston shimmered.

Minutes elapsed before silent contemplation shifted to that of sudden, decisive action. The driver killed the motor. Without the engine drone, the streets fell into complete silence. Nothing stirred until three of the four car doors opened and a trio of shadowy figures emerged. The threesome began walking along the ice-strewn pavement, maneuvering between waist-high snowbanks. As they drew nearer to their objective, their pace quickened. Moving swiftly now, foggy plumes of winter's breath escaped from their mouths. The men shielded their eyes as a sudden wind gust rippled along the street, buffeting road debris and loose snow.

Upon reaching the front of the apartment, the men paused at the leading edge of a narrow concrete walkway. The street behind them remained still. For the first time, words were spoken.

"That's the window I broke earlier," said one of the men – the crew's leader – in a low, muffled voice. He gestured toward a small, rectangular segment of cardboard that was taped over a gap in the glass panes encircling the door. His companions responded with a nod.

The spokesman then asked, "Are you guys ready for this?" Again, a simple nod.

Each of the three men reached into their jacket pockets and withdrew guns. Moonlight glinted off the brushed metal barrels.

The trio edged closer to the door. The leader, who had laid claim to the shattered window, reached for the cardboard and yanked it aside. He felt warm air escaping from inside. Extending his arm through the breach, he grasped the deadbolt. As he turned and disengaged the lock, it made a loud clicking noise. Pausing briefly, he listened for any sign of movement in the darkness. There was none.

Standing upright, he lowered his shoulder and threw his full weight into the door while twisting the knob. He stormed into the darkened foyer with his two accomplices trailing a half-step behind. As the men advanced, a guttural shout came forth from the lightless depths within.

"This is the police – drop your guns!"

It was a command that would trigger a torrent of deadly gunfire in the pitch-black apartment.

http://wbp.bz/sitda

 WILDBLUE
PRESS

See even more at:
http://wbp.bz/tc

More True Crime You'll Love From WildBlue Press

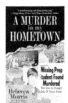

CPSIA information can be obtained
at www.ICGtesting.com
Printed in the USA
LVHW022156180219
607973LV00040B/992/P

9 781948 239929